BEING NORMAL IS THE ONLY WAY TO BE

WAYNE MARTINO is a Senior Lecturer in Education at Murdoch University, Perth, and before that he was a high-school English teacher for ten years. In mid 2005, he will take up a position at the University of Western Ontario, Canada. He is the author of several other books on education issues, especially as they relate to boys, including two previous titles with Maria Pallotta-Chiarolli, *Boys' stuff: Boys talking about what matters* and *So what's a boy? Addressing issues of masculinity and schooling*.

MARIA PALLOTTA-CHIAROLLI is Senior Lecturer in Social Diversity, Health and Education in the School of Health and Social Development, Deakin University, Melbourne. Aside from her previous co-authored books with Wayne Martino, her publications include *Girls talk: Young women speak their hearts and minds*, two autobiographical works, *Someone you know: An AIDS farewell*, *Tapestry: Five generations of women in an Italian family* and *When our children come out: How to support gay, lesbian, bisexual and transgendered young people*. Forthcoming books by Maria include *Border sexualities, border families in schools*.

We wish to dedicate this book to our vibrant young nieces who are all at the beginning of their schooling, in the hope that their lives at school may be healthy and happy!

Alessia and Daniella Chiarolli, Alix Farrally, Yasmin Martino, Deanna Pallotta and Paola Tatarelli.

Being normal is the only way to be

Adolescent perspectives on gender and school

WAYNE MARTINO
 and
MARIA PALLOTTA-CHIAROLLI

A UNSW PRESS BOOK

Published by
University of New South Wales Press Ltd
University of New South Wales
Sydney NSW 2052
AUSTRALIA
www.unswpress.com.au

©Wayne Martino & Maria Pallotta-Chiarolli 2005
First published 2005

This book is copyright. Apart from any fair dealing for the purpose of private study, research, criticism or review, as permitted under the Copyright Act, no part may be reproduced by any process without written permission. Inquiries should be addressed to the publisher.

National Library of Australia
Cataloguing-in-Publication entry

> Martino, Wayne.
> Being normal is the only way to be: adolescent perspectives on gender and school.
>
> Includes index.
> ISBN 0 86840 687 2.
>
> 1. Teenagers - Conduct of life. 2. Gender identity.
> 3. Sex differences in education. 4. School management and organization. I. Pallotta-Chiarolli, Maria. II. Title.
>
> 371.8

Design Di Quick
Cover image Di Quick
Printer Hyde Park Press

CONTENTS

Authors' note — vi
Acknowledgments — vii
Preface — ix
Introduction: Acknowledging student voice — 1

<u>1</u> BOYS AND SCHOOL: — 30
    'School sucks and the teachers are power freaks!'

<u>2</u> GIRLS AND SCHOOL: — 52
    'School is a pain in the butt'

<u>3</u> BEING A BOY: — 78
    'Guys can be like dogs and sniff you out fast'

<u>4</u> BEING A GIRL: — 95
    'It really all depends on what type of girl you are!'

<u>5</u> BOYS HARASSING GIRLS IN SCHOOL: — 122
    'Girls have it harder cos they have to deal with guys'

<u>6</u> 'BULLY BOYS' AND 'BITCH BARBIES': — 137
    Gender-based harassment in schools

<u>7</u> DEVELOPING STUDENT WELFARE POLICIES: — 162
    A whole school approach to gender and social justice

<u>8</u> CONCLUSION: — 171
    Questioning what it means to be 'really cool'

References — 183
Index — 191

AUTHORS' NOTE

The following key is used throughout this book to identify the quoted student's school, gender and age:

CCHS = Catholic co-educational school
GHS = government high school (Western Australia)
GHSV = government high school (Victoria)
RGHS = rural government high school
SSBS = single sex boys' school
SSGS = single sex girls' school

F = female student
M = male student

For example, GHSV F 94/16 would denote a female student, survey number 94, 16 years of age attending a government high school in Victoria.

ACKNOWLEDGMENTS

We wish to express our appreciation to the schools which allowed us to take up time and space in surveying so many students. Your commitment to promoting educational research and an e/quality of education is acknowledged.

We also wish to extend our appreciation and best wishes to the 900 young people who sat down with our surveys and wrote from their hearts and minds. We hope we have treated your words with respect, and done justice to you, your insights and lives.

Maria wishes to thank the incredible ongoing support and love of Rob and Steph Chiarolli. As Steph is now approaching the end of her schooling, this is a perfect time to acknowledge my appreciation of her insights and critiques of educational processes. Thanks for being the best Research Assistant/Key Informant anyone could ask for, Steph! But more importantly, thanks for your love, patience and inspiration!

Wayne would like to thank his partner, Jose Medeiros, and his parents for their support.

We also wish to thank our supportive colleagues and Heads of School at Deakin University and Murdoch University.

Finally, we would like to acknowledge our publisher John Elliot for his support and belief in this project. His feedback was significant in enabling us to develop the final product. It has also been a pleasure working with Heather Cam and Marie-Louise Taylor. We thank them for their attention to detail and patience. Di Quick's cover and page design has bought to life the energy of the young people with whom we have worked.

PREFACE

• SHE'S FIFTEEN. She used to get high grades and was really motivated until her so-called friends decided that she was no longer 'cool'. No boyfriend. She didn't talk about boys in the way they did and wouldn't even have one drink when they went to parties on the weekend. Putting on some weight didn't help either. Things got worse the day some boys noticed her school uniform stained with a small patch of blood as she returned to class after being granted permission to 'leave the room'. 'Period patch' they shrieked and burst into hysterical laughter as she walked by after class. It wasn't hard saying goodbye to her old friends because she had learned too quickly that they weren't really true friends, but she couldn't escape their bitchiness or the boys' cruel harassment that easily. She also became known as the dyke with the 'period patch'. Every morning when she woke up she felt that she wouldn't be able to endure another day. Plus her dieting had become so severe that she had started to feel weak and just found it difficult to concentrate in class sometimes. She also became good at living a lie at home. She would eat only to throw up afterwards in the toilet.

Meanwhile, her former friends are feeling other kinds of pressures – apart from having to look good, they are going to parties on the weekend, binge drinking, having unsafe sex, learning how to stay 'cool' and how to get a 'reputation'. They're not tight or frigid! It's not that easy being a girl, especially when boys and other girls start calling you a 'slut' behind your back.

But all schools offer compulsory Health and Sexuality education curriculum and have harassment policies, don't they? But to what extent are they adequately addressing these issues? To what extent is there a denial about the extent of such policing of sexuality and gender in young people's lives at school? After all, isn't this mainly about girls' 'out of school' behaviour which has no bearing on their learning?

Meanwhile, we're told by politicians and policymakers that girls are doing better than boys at school, that sex education has gone far enough, that girls are no longer victims of harassment.

• HE'S FOURTEEN, quiet, not into 'real' sport, loves reading, does dance classes. Some of the 'cool' boys call him 'gay', 'tampon-head', 'nerd'. One of his teachers, a late twenties 'cool' male teacher hired by the principal to be a role model to the boys, hears these cool boys talking like this but says nothing. They're just having a laugh, he rationalises. Another male teacher, also meant to be a role model for the boys, with the aim of encouraging them to read and write, allows a boy in the class to read out a verse of poetry. Since boys don't like writing poetry the teacher's strategy is to get the students to use their own language and to choose content that appeals to their peers. The class erupts into laughter as the boy reads his poem out aloud in a feigned exaggerated lisp. It's about a male student called 'tampon-head'. He has a boyfriend who is a ballet dancer. The teacher laughs, the students laugh. They're 'just being cool'. See, boys can really read and write. All they need is good male role models!

The quiet boy withdraws. He gets a reputation as a 'loner'. He just doesn't fit in with other boys. He should mix more with other boys, play a bit of football, just make more of an effort, some teachers tell his parents. He lacks social skills, they think. His parents receive his end-of-term report card and note his declining performance in several subjects. When the parents meet with the school counsellor and year co-ordinator, they are told their son is a 'fringe-dweller', 'immature', 'not mixing with the other boys in normal activities like football'.

Meanwhile, we're told by politicians and policymakers that we need male teachers in schools, that the 'feminisation' of schools has led to a 'crisis of masculinity', that boys' brains can't read or learn as well as girls so they need special programs and incentives like paying their parents to buy books, that sexual diversity is not to be discussed in schools, that homophobia is not such an issue in boys' lives at school as we are making it out to be.

'They're too scared to ask us what's really going on' or 'They just don't really want to know about what's really going on because then they would have to deal with the real issues', some students tell us. This book arose out of our ongoing frustration and incredulity at the widening chasm between what is happening to and for students in schools, and what right-wing backlash politicians and policymakers say is happening in schools and what needs to be done.

This book also arose out of our ongoing frustration and empathy with teachers and school counsellors who are working with the realities every day while framed and confined by the rhetoric of policy and politics.

Why don't we ask students what's happening in their lives at school? What are we afraid to hear? What will that mean for policy and politics? Are we invested in maintaining a schooling system constructed by adults, policed and framed by an adult culture based on misogynistic and heteronormative power and privilege? Why do we individualise the concern rather than address our school structures, policies and culture? And why do some teachers fear losing their jobs or their status if they dare to ask these questions?

So this is a book for teachers by students who worked with us to get their voices heard. Each chapter draws on the perspectives and writings of boys and girls and uses these to build up a specific knowledge about what it means to be a boy and a girl at school, what it means to be 'cool' and 'normal', and the effect of these social constructions on learning and relationships.

We deliberately foreground student voices and experiences so that you can explore and understand the social construction of gender and how it impacts on both girls' and boys' lives at school. This is important knowledge for teachers and those working in schools.

Student welfare or pastoral care policies in schools are silent about the effects of certain forms of gendered power relations on both learning and the social cultures of masculinity and femininity. Our intention is to make student voices and perspectives accessible to teachers in order to help build a threshold knowledge for teachers on gender and schooling.

At the end of each chapter we have included focus group discussions that are designed to function as Professional Development workshops or discussion forums for teachers. These workshops translate the content of the chapter into a form which can be applied to one's local school in order to generate deeper understandings about students' lives and experiences of gender. This culminates in a chapter that is devoted to providing guidelines for schools as a basis for recasting or reformulating their existing student welfare policies. What is provided here is a template for schools to work through a process of building a teacher threshold knowledge about gender diversity and schooling, and to articulate this in the form of a whole school based approach to addressing difference and interrogating what it means to be 'normal' or 'cool'.

We hope this book will be a useful resource for teachers and schools, and contribute in significant ways to further discussion about the gaps and silences in current school-based policies and approaches to addressing social justice, difference and diversity.

We also hope this book encourages you and provides practical support in undertaking your own research into the realities of your own school. Let's ask the students, let's question our adult cultures and investments, let's connect the rhetoric of policy to the reality of people, place and practice.

Wayne Martino
Murdoch University

Maria Pallotta-Chiarolli
Deakin University

INTRODUCTION:
Acknowledging student voice

When given the opportunity to write about their experiences at school, what do Australian students say? What do they tell us about the effects of what it means to be 'really cool'? How do their perspectives relate to current educational policies and practices in schools concerning 'pastoral care', addressing harassment and the commitment to creating safe schools? Based on what young people from different kinds of schools reported, this book provides insight into the impact of school cultures and structures on student relations and learning.

We wanted to give students the opportunity to write from a 'private' anonymous space where they were not subjected to the conventional forms of surveillance and policing from within the school and from teachers and their peers. In this sense, our work is grounded in a particular politics committed to hearing and recording the voices of young people (see also Pallotta-Chiarolli, 1998; Haag, 1999; Martino & Pallotta-Chiarolli, 2001). We believe that they have much to offer educators in terms of providing insight into improving the quality of learning and schooling (see Ancess, 2003; Lingard, B, Hayes, D, Mills, M & Christie, P, 2003). However, we are conscious that recording their voices is not entirely unproblematic and that researchers are implicated in a set of power relations that involve the authorisation of particular realities. Keeping this in mind, we are conscious of not wanting to colonise student voice in a way that subscribes to a tendency that masks the politics of knowledge production (Lather, 1990; Martino, 2003). As Trinh (1990) states:

2 Being normal is the only way to be

> no need to hear your voice when I can talk about you better than you can speak about yourself … I want to know your story. And then I will tell it back to you in a new way. Tell it back to you in such a way that it has become mine, my own, my re-writing you … I am still author, authority. I am still colonizer, the speaking subject and you are now at the center of my talk (343).

Thus we subscribe to an exploratory research process that involves a politics of commitment to hearing the voices of students which are often silenced in schools. What possibilities exist when spaces are created for students to express what they think and feel about their lives at school? Do they just provide us with what they think we want to hear? Is this just a space for a 'whine' or 'whinge' about school or is it an opportunity for students to produce their own knowledge about and insights into their own experiences of schooling? As Fine & Weis argue: 'For within the very centers of structured silence can be heard the most critical and powerful, if excluded, voices of teachers and students in public education' (2003: 69). And for the following students the exercise of writing about school was articulated in these terms:

- It's been good to vent/rant to you for a while. A bit of stress relief, really. Cya! (SSGS 1/15).

- Thank you for this survey. I need to let out some of my feelings … (CCHS M 14/16).

- It's school, what can I say? (GHSV F 73/15).

When given the opportunity to write about schooling in an anonymous way, what will students want to 'vent/rant'? Will they feel able to articulate their concerns and their affirmations in ways that they believe will be heard and listened to despite the 'very centers of structured silence' which frame students' lives at school through bureaucratic and institutional policy, curriculum and welfare decisions and implementations? Or are they resigned to having these structures define and determine their lives at school with minimal input from them and, indeed, what may appear to be minimal attention to them:

'what can I say?' One girl captured a feeling of desperate powerlessness and resignation reiterated by a number of students pertaining to the school culture failing to be a site for promoting safety and well-being:

- There are so many things to worry about at school that sometimes I feel that I need to depart this world. Expectations are very high whether it's required at school in the work you do or even in your friendship group to stop people talking badly about you ... I wanted to find a retreat in school but that failed as school is just like the outside world, just as nice and just as cruel (SSGS 159/16).

Thus, in this book, our aim is to present the perspectives of over 900 boys and girls in Australian schools on what life at school is like for them (see also Collins et al., 1996; Pallotta-Chiarolli, 1998; Haag, 1999; Martino & Pallotta-Chiarolli, 2001; Pallotta-Chiarolli, forthcoming, 2005a, 2005b). Through our open-ended questionnaire research, we wanted to give young people the opportunity to identify the issues that impact on them at school. Most students took up the opportunity with enthusiasm and wished us well:

- Good luck with your research! :) (GHSV F 208/16).

Indeed, they found the experience empowering:

- Thanks for listening/reading about the strange working of the mind of some random 16 year old girl. I'll now return to the 'real' world and bring about as much change as I possibly can (SSGS 157/16).

A few knew of our previous publications for young people (Pallotta-Chiarolli, 1998; Martino & Pallotta-Chiarolli, 2001) and were happy to be participating in research that would become part of future books:

- I really liked your books, really made you think about the bigger world (SSGS 62/16).

4   Being normal is the only way to be

A few tellingly felt that the exercise was futile, as if their perspectives wouldn't be heard or indeed change anything:

- School is great, fine, whatever. The experts can decide (GHSV F 94/16).

A few seemed to indicate that perhaps filling in surveys, being the researched, was a common (and non-productive?) tedium:

- The only problem [with school] is filling out crappy surveys like this one (GHSV M 140/16).

And of course, there were pragmatic reasons for appearing to be engrossed in this activity:

- I'm writing so much to take up time, I have Accounting next … (GSHV F 143/16).

Many students who participated in our research highlighted the impact of 'being normal' on their lives, which raises the urgent need for schools to address what it means to be 'really cool':

- Being 'Normal' is the only thing to be. You have to be in a way uniform because people want you to be that way, they try to make you like them, Average! Average everything, size, taste, friends, values, everything (CCHS M 6/15).

- I don't experience many problems at school. I just stick to what everyone else does, try not to stand out. That way you can't be criticised or hassled (CCHS M 5/14).

There appeared to be a sense of inevitability about this enforced normalisation as indicated by the following girl:

- Sometimes at school you wish that everybody looked the same and were nice to each other. But that's as likely as the school burning down (without a student lighting it) (CCHS F 172/15).

Such normalisation was often undertaken consciously through acts of self-surveillance and bodily comportment. The following boy highlights the power of self-regulation and all-embracing surveillance, dictated by the norms that have been internalised about how to walk as a 'normal boy':

> - As a boy you have to keep up an appearance such as how you think others see you and how you can alter that appearance ... I feel very conscious when walking through the school without friends because I'm not usually in a crowd and when walking through or past one it feels like everyone is staring at me. I'm fine when I'm talking to my friends but on my own I feel as if I walk lopsided and I try to walk as normally as possible (GHS M 226/14).

We believe that voices such as those above need to be heard as they are indicative of the range of reactions to education and educational authority. They also provide an insight into students' feelings of power, powerlessness and resistance both with regard to adult-centric structures and processes within a system which often does not acknowledge and even disregards their voices, and their positioning within a pecking order of peer group social relations involving what it means to be 'normal'.

Thus, we consciously authorise student voice and in so doing place students at the centre of our research. In this way, a space is created for students to draw educators' attention to the following issues:

- how hierarchies or pecking orders of masculinity and femininity impact on the lives of both girls and boys at school;
- how an exclusive focus on boys works to silence the very significant ways in which sexuality and gender continue to impact detrimentally on girls' lives at school;
- how homophobia impacts upon young people's peer group cultures and learning;
- how students critically question schooling in terms of its practices of normalisation;
- how many students are aware of and attempt to problematise the effects of gender and other influences in their lives at school.

An analysis of the above five themes is important given how the debates about boys' education that have been raging in Australia, the United Kingdom, the United States and New Zealand have tended to downplay the issues that continue to impact on girls at school (see Epstein et al., 1998; Gilbert & Gilbert, 1998; Kleinfield, 1998; Education Review Office, 1999; Francis, 1999; Collins et al., 2000; Hoff Sommers, 2000; Martino & Meyenn, 2001; Renold, 2001b; Kehily et al., 2002; McLeod, 2002; Titus, 2004; Weaver-Hightower, 2003). Weaver-Hightower (2003) refers to the shift in gender and education research as the 'boy turn'. He lists etiologies of the 'boy turn' in gender and education research: media panic, popular-rhetorical books, and news events; feminist examinations of gender roles; narrow initial indicators of gender equity; New Right and neoliberal reforms in education; explicit backlash politics; economic and workforce changes; parental concerns and pressure; and the 'thrill of the new' for researchers, educators and publishers (2003: 476). We want to counteract the powerful normalising tendency driving some of these etiologies and debates, and the positions taken up by those who advocate that boys are now being shortchanged (Kleinfield, 1998; see Lingard, Martino, Mills & Bahr, 2003 for a critique of these positions).

Backlash politics and politicians have constructed a discourse of the 'crisis in masculinity' in society, and schools are often seen as the sites of promulgation and percolation of this crisis (Mills, 2003). Although the uses of the term have varied, the 'crisis' commonly refers to 'perceptions that men in a society are acting in harmful ways toward themselves or others because of conditions in the culture, economy, or politics that prevent them from fulfilling a culturally specific "traditional" hegemonic masculine role', such as in educational sites (Weaver-Hightower, 2003: 478). However, research such as ours with young people in schools illustrates that this is little more than a diversionary debate that conceals what might be regarded as the 'real crisis of masculinity' that is still not being adequately addressed. Despite decades of consistent research findings about the prevalence and pertinence of homophobia and femiphobia, or the anxiety about homosexuality and discomfort with anything 'feminine', many educational policy-makers and administrators continue to deny the reality of how these sex/gender regimes impact on the social and learning cultures of schools (Ward, 1995; Laskey & Beavis, 1996; Robinson, 1996; Beckett, 1998; Duncan, 1999; Lipkin, 1999; Alloway, 2000; AAUW Legal Advocacy Fund, 2000; AAUW Educational Foundation, 2001; Martino & Pallotta-Chiarolli, 2003; Mills, 2004). In many research projects, students have repeatedly made educators and educational researchers aware that the real 'crisis in masculinity' is the misogynist reaction to any perception of so-called 'female' thinking and behaviour, the accepted hegemonic culture of male violence and power, and the fear many men in educational authority have of sexual diversity and non-hegemonic masculinities (Nayak & Kehily, 1996; Skelton, 1998, 2001; Mills, 2001; Dorais, 2004).

BACKLASH POLITICS AND GENDER REFORM

Thus, by not addressing the above mentioned frames of reference, boys are constructed as a homogenous group who are suffering as a result of the attention and resources committed to girls through feminist interventions in educational policy and practice (see Yates, 1997; Lingard, 2003). But, as Collins et al. (2000) have highlighted, factors such as socioeconomic status appear to be more significant when examining issues affecting the educational performance of students in schools. Working class girls and boys are still at risk in terms of educational attainment and literacy acquisition (see Alloway & Gilbert, 1997; Teese et al., 1997; Teese & Polesel, 2003). For example, Collins et al. (2000) have highlighted that even though boys' literacy skills are lower than those of girls, this does not translate into disadvantage in the same way as it does for girls in the post-school labour market (see also Weiner et al., 1997). Boys are still more likely to gain full-time employment than girls (see Rees, 1999). But certain boys and girls such as those from Indigenous backgrounds, poverty stricken backgrounds and working class boys are particularly disadvantaged in ways that white middle class boys are not.

Thus, the important question of 'which boys', 'which girls' is one that is not often addressed and this needs to be emphasised in any discussions about gender and educational disadvantage which presume that equal status for girls has been achieved at the expense of boys (see Kenway, 1995; Teese et al., 1997; Yates, 1997; Gilbert & Gilbert, 1998; Lingard & Douglas, 1999; Foster, 1998; Pallotta-Chiarolli, 1997; Foster et al., 2001). Foster, for instance, claims that while many women themselves find it easy to say they have achieved equality, 'that belief does not match up with the reality of most young women's lives' (1998: 82; see also Volman & ten Dam, 1999). It would appear that many of these backlash debates concerning boys are mainly about white, heterosexual, middle class, able-bodied boys (Martino & Meyenn, 2001). We would even go so far as to argue that the moral panic is driven by the need to preserve white heterosexual male privilege. This in turn, we would propose, is spurned on defensively by men under seige (Kenway, 1995) who perceive women to have achieved power and equality, while they themselves apparently have been left to struggle with an oppression ironically of their own making.

Both Lingard & Douglas (1999) and Petersen (2000) have drawn attention to the very significant role that 'recuperative masculinity politics' has played in driving men to react in very defensive ways at particular historical points in time to the power supposedly gained by women (see Faludi, 1991; Messner, 1997). Petersen argues that:

> the focus on physiological and gender dimorphism as the basis for a universal, normal erotic attraction, arose at a point in history when male dominance was coming under challenge ... (2000: 36).

He also claims, in drawing on the work of Laqueur (1990), that in the late eighteenth century this concentration on biological sex difference was:

> ... a response to the threat posed by the increasing demands of women to the dominant relations of gender following the rise of liberal democracy. Just as women were beginning to question the imperatives of marriage and motherhood, male political philosophers were beginning to argue that differences in women's and men's roles were rooted in immutable 'natural' differences (2000: 43–44).

Thus, such an emphasis on physiological and gender differences needs to be understood within the limits of quite specific sociocultural and historical frames of reference in which the emergence of backlash discourses against feminism have gained a particular currency (Faludi, 1991). As Petersen (2000) argues, historically:

> [m]ore and more, the emphasis was on defining natural differences between men and women which became the foundation for explaining and legitimating social differences (1998: 43).

For instance, an appeal to biological essentialism was used in the nineteenth century to establish the truth that women were intellectually inferior to men (see Alloway, 1995). The danger with such an appeal to essentialist discourses is the power invested in the truth claims that are generated in their capacity to normalise and homogenise populations, locating and fixing differential social practices and modes of thinking in gendered bodies and minds. The effects of reinforcing such gender dimorphism – intended or otherwise – are a definite demarcation of the normal versus the pathological or deviant gendered subject and, hence, the establishment of normative benchmarks for evaluating what constitutes masculinity and femininity on the basis of sexed bodies (see Foucault, 1978; Harding, 1998; Fausto-Sterling, 2000).

Currently we are witnessing a resurgence of bio-determinist explanations and justifications regarding boys' predisposed orientations to learning and behaviour (Gurian & Henley, 2001). This has led to advocating a more 'boy-friendly' curriculum, more male role models and single sex classes for boys to ameliorate the supposed feminisation of schooling (see Martino et al., 2004). This boys' education agenda needs to be understood within the broader context of anxiety and fear about the feminisation or 'pussification' of boys and men (du Toit, 2003), which is intensified by the emergence and increasing visibility of alternative forms of masculinity and empowered forms of femininity situated within a broader diversification of families, work and representations of gay, lesbian, bisexual, transgendered and other non-heterosexual subjectivities.

In this book, therefore, we highlight how the influences of gender normalisation, heteronormativity and other social influences feature in many boys' and girls' lives, with the capacity to impact in significant ways on their emotional, educational and mental health and well-being at school (see Collins et al., 1996; Kendall, 1996; Kendall & Walker, 1998; Goldflam et al., 1999; Collins et al., 2000; Dorais, 2004). We foreground the ways in which the debates about boys have worked to silence the impact of gender normalisation on the lives of girls, as well as to erase how questions of sexuality, geographical location, disability, race and ethnicity impact on students' lives at school (Mac an Ghaill, 1994; Walker, 1988; Pallotta-Chiarolli, 2000; Martino, 2003; Martino & Pallotta-Chiarolli, 2003). Moreover, what is highlighted are the very ways in which schools, as particular kinds of institutions, work to enforce a particular normalisation and surveillance which is rejected by many students. As the following student claims:

- School is like a prison. We are continuously moulded into shape. Filling our heads with useless info. We're treated like dumb beasts. We're forced into labour (GHSV F 108/15).

INTERROGATING THE PARLIAMENTARY INQUIRY INTO BOYS' EDUCATION

Within the backlash context of the debates about boys' education in Australia (Mills, 2003), a parliamentary inquiry into the education of boys was undertaken (House of Representatives Standing Committee on Education and Training, 2002). This report supports a 'recuperative masculinity politics', which involves constructing boys as the 'new disadvantaged' (Lingard & Douglas, 1999). Lingard, in fact, argues that the media has played a significant role in promoting this perspective and draws attention to its impact in setting the boys' educational agenda in a 'thinned out' gender equity policy context in Australia. He claims that 'the media constructions of backlash and especially in relation to boys as victims of schooling (Epstein et al.'s 'poor boys' discourse in the UK), become in a sense *de facto* policies for many self-managing schools and for many teachers, both male and female' (2003: 37).

The report advocates a recasting of the former National Gender Equity Policy to include a focus on 'positive values and goals' and 'quality teaching' (2002: v). It argues for a new policy framework to identify boys' and girls' 'common and separate educational needs'. What is overlooked in the current gender equity policy, according to the report, is 'the longer term impact of low achievement and the resulting restriction of some males to lower skilled employment'. Moreover, the report argues that changing labour markets are requiring different skills than those in the past, namely 'better communication and interpersonal skills', which boys, it claims, generally do not develop 'to the same extent as girls' (2002: xvii). This, it argues, has long-term implications for boys in terms of their entry and participation in the changing labour market. However, in the advocacy of 'quality teaching' and 'better communication and interpersonal skills', the report rejects the useful applications and understandings offered by those who argue for a focus on the social construction of gender. The question pertaining to *why* boys are reluctant to embrace such skills and capacities, and how schools might implement strategies to encourage them to develop a wider repertoire of skills, is not addressed.

Rather, what the report legitimates is 'taken for granted' and so-called 'common sense' understandings about the way boys behave and learn. This legitimation is then used to advocate a set of recommendations to address boys' educational needs such as:

- Boys need more explicit teaching than girls and tend to prefer more hands-on activities;
- Structured programs are better for boys because they need to know what is expected of them and moreover, they like to be shown the steps along the way to achieve success;
- Girls respond more readily to content while boys respond more to their relationships with teachers;
- Boys need activities;
- Boys respond better to teachers who are attuned to boys' sense of justice and fairness and who are consistent in the application of rules (2002: 78).

These kinds of claims are grounded in essentialised and 'common sense' understandings about the way boys learn or behave and ignore important research-based knowledge which points to more nuanced understandings about differences within groups of boys and within groups of girls (see Gilbert & Gilbert, 1998; Collins et al., 2000). What is left out in the report is a focus on the sex- and gender-based dimensions of bullying and violence in schools which impact on both marginalised boys and girls who are targeted by dominant boys and also by the dominant girls who aspire to some of the power gained via association and collusion with dominant boys at school (see Mills, 2001; Martino & Pallotta-Chiarolli, 2003). This omission is understandable given the particular backlash politics that drive the report, which aims to convince the public that boys are truly the 'new disadvantaged'. For instance, it states that, 'The assumption in recent decades appears to have been that girls have urgent educational needs to be addressed and that boys will be all right' (2002: xvi) and, hence, supports the populist belief that there has been a decided attempt to deny the reality of boys' educational and social disadvantage in schools. In light of this, the following evidence is provided to 'set the record straight' and to lay the claim that 'there is justification for many of the concerns about boys' education' (2002: xv):

- Measures of early literacy achievement: in 2000, 3.4% fewer Year 3 boys and 4.4% fewer Year 5 boys achieved national benchmarks than girls.
- School retention: for boys to Year 12, retention rate was 11% lower than that for girls in 2001.
- Girls are achieving higher average marks in the majority of subjects at Year 12 and the gap between boys and girls has continued to widen.
- Admission to higher education: 56% of university entrance applicants are women but this is balanced by higher rates of participation in post-school VET by males.

However, Collins et al. argue, in an earlier report entitled *Factors influencing the educational performance of males and females in school and their initial destinations after leaving school*, that:
- Girls are less likely to secure full-time employment, and more likely to be involved in undertaking activities which put them out of the labour market.

- The way the structure of Year 12 assessment privileges some combinations of subjects and certain subjects, works to disadvantage girls.
- The fact that girls in general have an order of literacy skills does not give them better labour market outcomes than boys.
- Boys' participation in a narrow and vocationally oriented range of school subjects may mean they miss out on opportunities to develop diverse knowledge and skills, including interpersonal and civic skills, and to foster their social and cultural capacities. However, it does not mean they are disadvantaged with regard to employment.
- Girls may stay on longer at school than boys do, but this is necessary to secure opportunities for employment and post-school studies. Girls are disadvantaged if they leave early and are much more likely than boys not to be in full-time employment.
- Boys who leave school before completing Year 12 are only 4% less likely to have full-time work at around age 24 than those who completed Year 12 but did not complete further major tertiary qualifications. Girls who leave before completing Year 12 are 21% less likely to be in full-time employment than girls who complete Year 12 but do not complete further major qualifications.
- Girls' overall higher average performance in most subjects in Year 12 does not translate into better labour market outcomes for all girls. In the seven years following Year 12, recent ACER (Australian Council for Educational Research) research indicates that while males are more likely than females to be registered in the official unemployed category, they are also considerably more likely to be in training schemes leading safely to full-time work, and considerably less likely to be permanently in the part-time employment labour market or to be out of the labour force altogether.
- More females than males enter higher education. Much of this difference results from mature-age female entrants in their twenties, not from large differences in the proportions of school leavers of each gender entering directly from school. School leavers proceeding to university immediately or after one year's break from study now make up only around 35% of entrants to undergraduate programs in Australian universities (2000: 3, 7).

What is often ignored when boys are constructed as the 'new disadvantaged' are other details about participation and subject choice, which provide a more nuanced perspective on gender and schooling. For instance, information about girls' 'under-enrolment' in the highest level maths, physics, economics and information technology subjects is usually not included. This is consistent with the review of literature undertaken by Sukhnandan et al. in the United Kingdom which reveals that girls 'tend to underestimate their own ability' (2000: 11) which Collins et al. (2000) suggest may be one of the reasons why girls tend to steer away from participating in higher level mathematics courses.

Given the silences or erasure surrounding girls' experiences of and participation in schooling within the context of these debates, we wanted to provide students with the opportunity – both boys and girls – to write about life at school. Our purpose was to investigate the extent to which their experiences correlate with how policies and backlash debates about boys' education are constructing and circumscribing the terms of reference for reformulating current gender equity policy and discourse (Lingard, 2003; Mills, 2003; Martino et al., 2004).

ABOUT THE STUDY

Students aged 14–16 (Year 10 and Year 11) from six Australian schools responded to an extended response survey question. They were asked to write about what life at school as a boy or as a girl was like, to highlight what they enjoyed about school, and to describe any problems they experienced. As stated at the beginning of this introduction, our major aim was to give young people the opportunity to 'speak their hearts and minds', and to enable their voices to be heard by the very people who are positioned as experts and authorities in adolescent health and education (see Le Compte, 1993; Martino & Pallotta-Chiarolli, 2001). We also wanted to explore the interdependencies, complexities and multi-directionality of the five issues listed toward the beginning of this introduction, and thereby resist a simplistic, singular and homogenising approach to the study of gender in education.

Thus, in order to explore gender relations, hierarchies and interdependencies, we wanted to avoid research that was only with boys or only with girls, thereby sustaining an oppositional binary construction of gender and divorcing it from other interwoven social determinants such as class, ethnicity and geographical location. Although acknowledging the importance and efficacy of single sex research, as we ourselves have found in the past (Pallotta-Chiarolli, 1998; 2000; Martino & Pallotta-Chiarolli, 2001; 2003), we believed that in order to address the gaps and silences driving gender debates at policy and ministerial level, particularly in relation to how girls' educational and sociocultural needs are being constructed as historical concerns no longer relevant in today's schools, we needed to understand and explore gender in complexly interrelated ways that avoid the 'girls then, boys now' temporally linear discourse (Weaver-Hightower, 2003). Our challenge, as set by Weaver-Hightower, was 'How might we research and write about boys and girls within the same article or book?' (2003: 479). Thus, given these aims and concerns, the following schools from various socioeconomic locations and with both single sex and co-educational groupings were chosen:

- a single sex boys' school in a high socioeconomic suburb in Perth, Western Australia (SSBS/ $n = 69$);
- a rural government high school in a low socioeconomic area in New South Wales (RGHS/ $n = 40$: 22 boys, 18 girls);
- a Catholic co-educational school in a middle class suburb in Perth (CCHS/ $n = 260$: 149 boys, 111 girls);
- a government high school in a low socioeconomic suburb in Perth (GHS/ $n = 223$: 101 boys, 122 girls);
- a government high school in a middle socioeconomic suburb in Melbourne, Victoria (GHSV) $n = 221$: 106 boys, 115 girls);
- a single sex girls' school in a high socioeconomic suburb in Melbourne (SSGS/ $n = 171$).

We were concerned to gain a cross-section of students from various social class locations and to document the ways in which they constructed their experiences of schooling. What emerged for many students was an overwhelming rejection of schooling in relation to both learning and the school culture, and indeed an identification and understanding of the inter-relatedness of these two dimensions. This connection between social and school cultures of gender, sexuality and learning is what has been largely omitted from parliamentary debates and policy-making where learning has been constructed as separate and unaffected by sociocultural frameworks and constructions.

The majority of respondents made very critical comments about the overall culture of the school with its narrow emphasis on the policing, surveillance and disciplining of students. They were also very critical of the normalisation that infiltrated many boys' and girls' social relationships and modes of relating to one another. In fact, both boys and girls highlighted the gendered and sex-based dimensions of the social hierarchies of peer group relationships at school and the effects of these on their emotional and mental health and well-being, as well as on their capacity and ability to participate in learning (see Blackmore et al., 1996; Collins et al., 1996; Fitzclarence et al., 1996; Kehily & Nayak, 1997). In fact, many students commented on the gendered dimensions of bullying and its effects on the lives of both boys and girls who failed to measure up to the norms for performing or 'doing' desirable masculinity and femininity (see Ward, 1995; Boulden, 1996; Butler, 1996; Nickson, 1996; Pallotta-Chiarolli, 1998; Duncan, 1999; Alloway, 2000; Mills, 2001; Martino & Pallotta-Chiarolli, 2003; Dorais, 2004).

While these issues have already been documented effectively and extensively by others (Frank, 1993; Lees, 1993; Mac an Ghaill, 1994; Nayak & Kehily, 1996; Salisbury & Jackson, 1996; Epstein, 1997; Hey, 1997; Walker, 1998; Davison, 2000), we are concerned to highlight once again how first, such gender regimes continue to impact in significant ways on the lives of boys and girls at school despite their various class locations; and second, the ongoing erasure and silencing of these issues in public debates around the need to address boys' educational and social needs. Moreover, we are interested to draw out the implications of how students construct their experiences of schooling for teachers and school leaders who, *in loco parentis*, are invested with a particular responsibility and duty of care for ensuring the well-being of all students at school (see Ward, 1995; Butler, 1996; Laskey & Beavis, 1996; Nickson, 1996; Becket, 1998; Letts & Sears, 1999; Alloway, 2000).

AN OVERVIEW OF THE RESULTS

Across all schools, similar issues arose for students. In making sense of the data, certain categories were used to explore patterns in the way that the students were responding to the survey questions. While it is acknowledged that these categories of analysis are a result of the arbitrary decisions made by us as researchers and are governed by certain norms, we are upfront about acknowledging the feminist and cultural studies frames of reference which enable us to interpret the data in this way (Lather, 1990; Gaztambide-Fernandez et al., 2004). As we were reading the surveys, we indicated certain topics or issues which students tended to raise repeatedly and this was bracketed according to the following themes depending on the school:

- rejecting school and teachers;
- pressure of exams and school work;
- drugs and alcohol at school;
- problems created by other boys/girls and peer group related issues;
- specific issues related to bullying and harassment at school as a result of socialisation into peer group hierarchical cultures at school.

What arises for us in analysing the data, given the backlash context of the debates which have focused on differential performance of boys and girls at school, are the health-related issues impacting on the mental health and well-being of students – such as the prevalence and effects of homophobia in boys' lives, and the role that body (its weight, image and menstrual function) and sexual relations with boys plays in how girls fashion their femininities (see Steiner-Adair, 1991; Haag, 1999; Tanenbaum, 2002). We were interested in the panopticonic or all-embracing gaze whereby these issues were not only invisibilised, but self-policed. Foucault (1978) explains how the panopticonic prison placed one guard in the centre who watched all the prisoners day and night. One effect of constantly being watched, or believing that they were constantly being watched, was that 'prisoners began to watch themselves'. The guard's gaze was 'internalized in each prisoner, who took on the responsibility to supervise himself. The panoptical gaze is the self-surveillance of those who have been conditioned to being watched, evaluated, and measured. The panoptical gaze produces control through normalization' (Lesko, 2000: 111). The processes of normalisation, self and other policing and regulation, and the performance of an appropriate gender, were clearly evident in young people's responses in our survey.

SINGLE SEX BOYS' SCHOOL (SSBS)

What was interesting about the way many boys responded at this affluent single sex school was their rejection of the institutionalised culture of masculinity that was manifested for them in terms of the prevalence of homophobia and bullying endemic in hierarchical peer group relations, the school's emphasis on sport, the formal, traditionalist approach to teaching, discipline and the emphasis on uniform (see Jackson, 1998; White, 2004). Thirty-three boys (47.8%), for example, made some critical comment about the old-fashioned approach to teaching and often viewed learning at school as out of touch with their everyday lives in the outside world. As the two following boys stated emphatically: 'Boys deal with Homophobes' (SSBS 7/16); 'Some boys get called poofs – that's an issue!' (SSBS 6/15). Many made reference to oppressive power in the following terms: 'Life at school is like living in a Nazi camp. With the exception of a few teachers most are Hitler's followers with the attitude that they, the teacher, can never be wrong!' (SSBS 2/16). Another significant number of the cohort (26 boys or 37.6%) also drew attention to the issue of boys feeling compelled to act 'cool' and mentioned how homophobia and the requirement to measure up to the stereotypes of macho masculinity posed a particular problem for boys in terms of how they related in peer group situations.

Interestingly, the homophobia in the single sex school situation appeared to be intensified with a number of boys expressing concern about whether there might be same-sex attracted or gay boys at their school. In fact, 10 boys (14.5%) made specific reference to homophobia or expressed some form of homophobia. At times this preoccupation with gay sexuality was manifested in 'humorous' fictitious accounts of boys visiting the headmaster's office where homosexual acts would be performed. This use of sexuality in humour appeared to be a means by which some boys were able to disrupt and subvert the authority of the school in its imposition of what was perceived to be a strict regime of power and conformity limiting unnecessarily the boys' freedom.

SINGLE SEX GIRLS' SCHOOL (SSGS)

Many of the girls in this affluent school wrote positively about their experience of school and spoke of the commitment of their teachers. Unlike the boys attending the single sex boys' school, only 21.6% of the cohort (37 girls) made some critical comment about the teachers being too strict or enforcing 'stupid rules' and about school not being relevant. Overall, there was a sense that school was an affirming and positive place, with only 7% (12 students) of the cohort indicating that they disliked or hated school. In fact, 14.6% (25 girls) indicated that there were no problems for them at all and that they loved school. Many of these girls emphasised their involvement in extracurricula activities and sport. However, while 59.6% (102 girls) of the cohort indicated they liked school, they did qualify this by identifying particular issues or problems that impacted on them at school. 62.5% referred to bitchiness, fitting in, and 'rich, stuck up anorexic bitches' (also referred to as 'Britney Spears clones') as major problems for them at school. 23.3% (40 girls) mentioned specifically body weight/image and appearance as significant issues impacting on the quality of their lives at school. Two girls stated that they had attempted suicide and undertaken self-harming in the past due to feeling inadequate and isolated, while one girl indicated that the thought occasionally crossed her mind when she considered the overwhelming demands on her life to succeed in all ways.

Interestingly, 26% (44 girls) emphasised that they found it easier being in a girls' school because the absence of boys translated into school being a more safe and comfortable place for them where they did not have to worry about the way they looked or impressing boys. However, there were contradictions for at least two of the girls who argued that while they did not have to worry about 'having to impress the boys', they asserted that there was still the pressure to have 'the right clothes' etc. Thus there appeared to be certain practices of self-monitoring that were dictated by the gaze and surveillance of boys, but equally another set of self-regulatory practices dictated by the girls and centred around body image and appearance. What was also interesting about this latter issue of harassment and hierarchy between girls was the number of times it was related to/connected to boys outside the school who the girls were in friendships and relationships with. Thus, although not physically present as regulators, boys' expectations and the hierarchy of femininities constructed by dominant masculinity were not absent: they still impacted upon girls and were indeed policed by girls (Duncan, 2004). Other girls (15% or 26 girls) indicated that not having boys at school was a problem and associated this absence with intensified 'bitchiness' amongst the girls. Interestingly, the presence of boys appeared to function for many of these girls as a regulatory force in diminishing the latter's tendency to engage in 'bitchiness'.

RURAL GOVERNMENT HIGH SCHOOL (RGHS)

Certain patterns also emerged in the rural lower socioeconomic status (SES) government high school for both boys and girls but more so in terms of their *protest* against the institutionalised regimes of power, authority and pedagogy enacted by teachers. However, due to the sample size, it is not possible to make generalisable claims about students' overall experiences in rural schools. It is interesting to note that almost half of the boys (45.5%) and just over half of the girls (55.5%) made some critical comment about teachers and/or the restrictive nature of schooling in terms of its lack of flexibility and irrelevancy to their own lives in the outside world. The tendency with the single sex boys continues with 7 boys (31.8%) also identifying their male peers as perpetrating homophobia and other antisocial practices related to the need to prove their masculinity. Over half the girls (55.5%) identified 'bitchiness' and body image/weight issues as constituting major problems for them in their relationships with other girls at the school. The policing of femininities in terms of the body and the 'bitchiness' amongst girls was at the basis of hierarchies that existed amongst girls at school. In fact, the popular girls were the 'pretty girls' who had gained the status of popularity defined and regulated, it appeared, by the popular boys. This became even more apparent with 33.3% of the girls mentioning the issue of boys hassling girls at school and how their femininity and sexuality were policed through sexist regimes of practice involving the inevitable trap of being caught within the Madonna/whore binary. In other words, they felt the gaze of boys fixing their subjectivities through a set of power relations which led them to be perceived as 'sluts' if they engaged in sexual relations with boys and 'tight bitches' if they chose not to (see Lees, 1993; Hey, 1997). Boys continue to pose major problems for girls in terms of this sex-based harassment and policing of girls' femininity – issues which are somehow invisibilised in the debates about boys.

Another interesting point to note was that 4 rural boys mentioned suicide. These boys talked about their feelings of isolation, which were often the result of other boys engaging in exclusionary practices of masculinity that involved repudiating those boys who failed to measure up to what was considered to be cool or socially desirable male behaviour.

CATHOLIC CO-EDUCATIONAL HIGH SCHOOL (CCHS)

In this middle class school a similar pattern also emerges for both boys and girls in terms of the frequency of their disparaging comments about teachers/school in general and the effects of peer group pressures and conformity. 44.2% of boys and 37.8% of girls mentioned their dissatisfaction with schooling and teachers, time after time drawing attention to the school's emphasis on enforcing rigid disciplinary practices as opposed to encouraging the student body to engage in an active dialogue with teachers and administrators regarding school management issues. This school, for the most part, was constructed by students as insular and, from our reading of their scripts, appeared to subscribe to 'traditional and hierarchical versions of power and of masculinity' (Collins et al., 2000: 101). This appeared to be one of those schools identified by Collins et al. (2000) which:

- operated mainly at the level of hyper-rationality, discipline and control, avoiding empathic and affiliative behaviours;
- were repressive in their teacher/student relations and did not offer their students opportunities to develop wise judgements or to exercise their autonomy in responsible ways (101) (see also Kenway et al., 1997).

In this school 40.9% of boys and 72% of girls also mentioned peer pressure and peer group relations involving bullying as impacting significantly on their lives at school. Almost every girl indicated that 'bitchiness' was a major social problem for her in her relationships with other girls. This was exacerbated for many (36%) by the added dimension of sex-based harassment and sexist practices perpetrated by the boys.

GOVERNMENT HIGH SCHOOL (GHS)

The results for this lower SES government high school in Western Australia are similar to those of the Catholic high school. 63.4% of boys and 55.7% of girls were very critical of teachers and school overall. Like students in the other schools, they identified oppressive forms of power such as enforcing strict rules and teachers' lack of flexibility as unnecessarily limiting their freedom: 'At our school we have a 6 ft barbed wire fence all way around and teachers walk around with walkie-talkies and tell us how to dress and they think they're superior to us just because they're staff' (GHS M 234/15). 39.6% of boys wrote about peer group practices of masculinity in terms of bullying, homophobia and acting 'cool': 'Boys at school have to maintain their macho image in front of all the other boys and sometimes this can lead to bullying and fighting' (GHS M 223/15). This was also exemplified by the following boy's comment: 'Boys are faced with the dilemma that they have to live up to their friends' expectations and not their own, i.e. they have to be macho and brutal all the time when in actual fact they aren't, but if they don't act like that they are considered a faggot or gay!!!!' (GHS M 269/16). However, an overwhelming 57.4% of girls mentioned 'bitchiness' and body weight issues as a problem in their lives at school and this emerged as a constant problem for girls across all schools in our study: 'I have to say that there's a lot of bitchiness and a quest to be popular between the girls at our school' (GHS F 22/16). 35.2.% also commented on sex-based harassment and teasing from boys: 'I honestly think that the boys are immature and tend to hassle a lot of girls and this does cause problems' (GHS F 11/15). Four girls (3.2%) also mentioned the issue of suicide. Interestingly, both boys and girls mentioned the impact of certain boys in terms of their disruptive or 'immature' behaviour in class and its effect on their ability to concentrate.

GOVERNMENT HIGH SCHOOL (GHSV)

Overall, both boys and girls at this middle class school indicated that they liked school but stated that there were some problems (30 boys or 28% and 48 girls or 41.7%). For all students the major problem related to the stress associated with increased workload and expectations to achieve with the transition into Year 11 (33 boys or 31% and 35 girls or 30.4%). More boys than girls tended to state that school was boring (22% of the boys as opposed to 13% of the girls). Both boys and girls emphasised the social dimension of schooling in terms of being with friends as a significant positive aspect (17% or 18 boys and 22.6% or 26 girls). Interestingly, 16% (17) of the boys made the point that it was better being a boy at school or that it was easy for them being a boy at school. Almost equal numbers of boys and girls indicated that they strongly disliked school (15 girls or 13% and 11 boys or 10%) or that there were no problems at all for them at school (25 girls or 21.7% and 22 boys or 20.7%). Similar numbers also identified teachers as being a problem (16 girls or 14% and 11 boys or 10%).

A number of boys mentioned that having to impress girls or that they were 'cock teasers' was a problem for them (13% or 14 boys), while others affirmed the possibility of being in a school where 'chicks' were available (5% or 5 boys). Another distinctive element or pattern emerging in some of the boys' responses was their tendency to use humour, sexuality and sexism in a manner consistent with performing hegemonic heterosexual masculinity (7% or 7 boys). It may be that these boys were performing for their peers given that the survey was administered in an auditorium at the school where students were packed closely together, some of them sitting on the floor. For example, one boy talked about the boy next to him who he claimed 'gets sexually harassed' by a teacher and then adds that he is joking at the end of the survey. A different boy talks about teachers 'picking him up' because he is 'sexy'. Another claims that his sexual frustration is so great that he 'fantasises about raping people'. One boy claims that he likes school because he 'gets lots of free sex' while another talks about how difficult school can be because 'it is hard being a homosexual with a small penis'. Given the context, these narratives may be understood as produced to shock the researcher. However, they are equally significant in terms of their potential to function as a means by certain boys in these circumstances to assert a particular form of hegemonic heterosexual masculinity that is mobilised through sexist, homophobic and sexualised discourses under the normalising gaze of other boys.

Equal numbers of girls (13%) also stated that boys posed a problem for them either in terms of their immature and disruptive behaviour in class or in terms of their harassing behaviours. However, 15.6% of girls also identified 'fitting in' or 'bitchiness' to be a problem amongst girls. 13% specifically mentioned body image and/or appearance to be a problem in relating to their peers at school. However, many more girls had a tendency to assert that there were no special issues that just boys or just girls had to deal with at school (26% or 30 girls as opposed to 6% or 6 boys).

Overall, across most of the schools we surveyed, there was an overwhelming emphasis on the sex-based and gendered dimensions of harassment for boys and girls at school which impacted significantly on their lives. The other major issue for many students also related to the regulatory normalising practices and codes of behaviour enforced by schools to ensure conformity to what we consider to be white middle class norms. In short, many students felt that their school was out of touch with their everyday lives and rejected what they perceived to be culturally irrelevant practices and knowledges (see Pallotta-Chiarolli, 1998; Walker, 1988; Martino & Pallotta-Chiarolli,

2001). The only exception appeared to be the single sex girls' school where many of the girls wrote about school being a safe place where they were supported by teachers and embraced learning. However, there were many girls who emphasised the problem of surveillance by their peers in relation to body image and appearance and who also spoke of intensified regimes of bitchiness amongst the girls. They also mentioned the power exerted by the 'rich' 'snobbish' girls as a problem leading to hierarchical peer group dynamics at the school.

What these students have to say has definite implications for improving social and pedogogical relations in schools. In the following chapters we analyse specific comments written by students to draw out further how particular gender issues impacted on their experiences of schooling and social relationships with their peers. We do this in order to articulate for teachers/schools what this means for developing school-based policy and practice through discussion forums which engage with the issues and concerns raised by the students.

There are two further issues that need to be addressed as they point to our specific framing of the categories informing our analysis of the data. First, there is a caution around our use of the word 'bitchiness'. There has been some debate among feminists and educators regarding the gendered and possibly trivialising usage of the term 'bitchiness' to define a form of bullying perpetuated by girls toward their female peers (see Tanenbaum, 2002). In the light of our research methodology, which aims to use and present the voices and perspectives of young people, and given that the term 'bitchiness' is commonly used by the girls themselves to delineate a particular form of harassment and intimidation between girls, we have decided to utilise this term and elaborate upon its use and manifestations in later chapters: 'While boys are given permission to punch and kick to express negative feelings, girls are taught to avoid direct conflict ... Many girls master the hidden machinations of indirect aggression' (Tanenbaum, 2002: 43). Thus, various methods of exclusion and intimidation are undertaken through gestures, territoriality, rumouring, and the strategic use of silence. Although our use of the word 'bitchiness' may be taken to be undermining the damage and efficacy of such methods of harassment and bullying, this is certainly not our intention. We use this term because it is utilised by girls, and some boys, to identify the specific forms of intra-gender insider/outsider boundary-delineation practices. In short, our use of this word is indicative of our commitment to reporting and presenting the everyday realities of schooling via the language that students themselves use.

A second issue which frames the following chapters is one that is often pointed out to us by students in schools when we conduct research and/or facilitate workshops and seminars with them. It is also one that we believe is not addressed by backlash educational agendas. Students inform us that they wish to tell educational researchers and policy-makers: 'Stop blaming us, we didn't create this culture, and check out what you're like'. They are quick to point out gendered, homophobic and risk-taking behaviours such as involving drugs and alcohol in adults, indeed in their parents' peer groups: 'It's not just teenagers that dish out peer group pressure'. In the words of academics who explore the social, political and historical construction of adolescence, adolescents are not outside society and history. There is a 'dominant set of assumptions and ideas – what is called the "discourse of Adolescence" [which] affects and influences all adolescents' lives' (Lesko, 2000: 11–12; see also Harris, 2004). Adolescence is 'racialized, gendered, and nationalized' and we would add, commodified. Indeed, social theorists such as Lesko believe that 'the adolescent' is a convenient political focus, 'always ready to indicate and exemplify national crises, and a perfect trope for worry, study, and action-taking that also met the coming-of-age interests of white middle class professionals', and thereby preventing the normative gaze being turned back onto the social adult cultures wherein lie the real concerns, impetus and politico–economic manipulations of young people (2000: 47; see also Harris, 2004). In undertaking this research, and yet again turning the spotlight onto various adolescents, we wish the reader to keep in mind how the discursive construction of adolescence acts as:

> a trope for … [national] worries about unknown futures, about ability to succeed and dominate in changing circumstances, about maintenance of gender and class hierarchy in changing social and cultural landscapes … adolescence can be glimpsed as a technology to produce certain kinds of persons within particular social

arrangements [that perform necessary functions in] broader cultural debates about knowledge, identity, representation, and power. In other words, adolescent bodies became a terrain in which struggles over what would count as an adult, a woman, a man, rationality, proper sexuality, and orderly development were staged (2000: 50).

For example, adults within educational systems often fail to understand their own investments in the success of certain adolescent groupings in a school, typically white middle class heterosexual boys, or as Lesko states more bluntly, 'typically the Jocks' (2000: 187). And, although we asked for individual responses in our research about individual experiences, we wanted to see and understand collective social practices as well as individual responses to broader social contexts. Attention to 'the specific agency and meaning-making of individuals, but always within the collectively identified and historically provided contexts and range of possibilities' (Lesko, 2000: 194) framed our research aims and methods.

Finally, in order to facilitate teacher engagement with student voice, we have provided a set of focus questions at the end of each chapter. These questions can serve as a basis for setting up Professional Development forums in schools to enable educators to reflect further on the relationship between policy and practice as it pertains to student welfare issues in their own schools (see Darling-Hammond, 1997; Ancess, 2003).

GENERAL OR OVERARCHING CONCEPTS

AIM • To build an overall understanding about the impact of gender on boys' and girls' lives at school

HIERARCHIES OF MASCULINITY AND FEMININITY

There are different ways of being a boy and a girl. These are influenced by the way students act, how they talk, what they talk about, their appearance, their peer group.

FOR REFLECTION
- What does the word 'hierarchy' highlight?
- Consider what 'being cool' might mean to a boy and girl at school. What are the similarities/differences?
- Are there pecking orders amongst various groups of boys and girls at school?
- How might you account for these differences?

HOMOPHOBIA AND FEMIPHOBIA

Homophobia and femiphobia impact on many boys' lives at school. Homophobia refers to the fear of gay boys or those who are perceived to be gay. It is important to make this distinction. Femiphobia refers to the fear of the feminine or any association with what is considered to be feminine.

FOR REFLECTION
- Why do you think it is important to draw the distinction between homophobia and femiphobia?
- What is the link between the two?

HETEROSEXISM AND COMPULSORY HETEROSEXUALITY

Heterosexism is the belief or the unquestioned assumption that everyone is heterosexual. It involves a denial and often a blatant refusal of same-sex orientation. Compulsory heterosexuality refers to the requirement to present oneself as appropriately heterosexual.

FOR REFLECTION
- Why is it important to name heterosexism as a powerful form of discrimination?
- How is this manifested for boys and girls at school?
- What do they do to assert their heterosexuality?

NORMALISATION

Normalisation refers to the processes and influences that result in people thinking of themselves as 'normal'. These are always culturally and historically specific.

FOR REFLECTION
- What assumptions or expectations often influence the way many people think about what it means to be a boy or a girl?
- Are boys and girls expected to behave in different ways in certain situations/contexts?
- What happens if a boy transgresses or fails to measure up to these social expectations?
- What are the consequences for girls?

POLICING MASCULINITY AND FEMININITY

Policing is about surveillance of other people. It involves both boys and girls monitoring one another and deciding what is appropriate or inappropriate, who is to be included or excluded, what is 'cool' or 'uncool'.

FOR REFLECTION
- What does the word 'policing' highlight?
- How does this idea of policing relate to social hierarchies and marginalisation in young people's lives at school?

1

BOYS AND SCHOOL:
'School sucks and the teachers are power freaks!'

• The teachers have no idea how to teach, yes they know how to 'teach', that is by the book but no teacher can reach out to students anymore ... I don't want to learn and they don't want to teach. Our education system is completely screwed ... teachers have really squeezed this term till it's dry ... No I am not a troublemaker. I sit in class and do what I'm told but inside I long for more. School has crushed my dreams. On this day I honestly have no idea where life is taking me. I'm crawling in the dark and I just wish someone could turn on the light (GHSV M 97/16).

IN THIS CHAPTER YOU WILL:

• learn more about what boys really think about school and teachers;

• develop a greater understanding about the structures and approaches to teaching and learning that boys are critical of;

• engage in a Professional Development session using boys' voices to build knowledge about effective schooling for boys.

INTRODUCTION

In this chapter, via the narratives of individual students, we focus on the following two themes found in our research: boys' engagement with and critical interrogation of school structural and pedagogical processes. However, as will become evident, these themes cannot be detached from sociocultural discourses of class, gender and sexuality, particularly middle class compulsory heterosexuality and misogyny. Our research showed that many students – both boys and girls – were very critical of a particular form of power that teachers exercised and which was legitimated by the hierarchical structure of the school itself. They did not appear to be rejecting teacher authority per se, but rather were vehemently opposed to the ways in which teachers deployed their authority.

REJECTING AUTHORITARIAN POWER STRUCTURES

For boys across all surveyed schools there was a rejection of impositional and authoritarian hierarchical power structures. This was often manifested in their comments about teachers' uses and abuses of power and frequent references to the school's emphasis on regulatory and inflexible supervisory procedures for managing student behaviour (see Symes & Meadmore, 1996). This is captured by the following boy's response from the single sex boys' school:

- The teachers reckon they deserve respect without earning it. Good teachers are hard to come by ... The whole discipline system is wrong as well, there is no incentive to do well for people like myself. Creativity is stifled by the rules. Schools like this are trying to churn out generic people, devoid of personality. The teachers, in a lot of cases, are a huge problem. They make up their own rules, constantly put students down, dish out punishments if they're having a bad day. The school also invades way too far into the private lives of the students (SSBS 1/16).

This boy draws attention to four hierarchical oppositional binaries at work that prevent the facilitation of a school environment conducive to promoting learning and satisfying interpersonal relations. These involve: the teacher versus student hierarchy; the emphasis on discipline by teachers decreasing the motivation to learn among students; the emphasis on rules eroding creativity; and the blurring of students' boundaries between what they consider to be their public selves that teachers can engage with, and their private selves that teachers intrude into.

Many boys such as the following highlight the role that school plays in enforcing certain practices of normalisation of which they are very critical. They appear to be rejecting the ways in which they are regulated at school and compelled to conform to normative standards of conduct, enforced through what Hunter (1994) has termed a supervisory technology of moral surveillance:

- Our school uniform is gay, it makes people look like boy scouts. Ties have to be worn constantly and socks pulled up to knee height … We supposedly have a say in what the school does but they don't listen and they don't care … I am against the power that the school holds us under. I get in shit for everything and have people watching my fucking back every minute of the day (SSBS 9/17).

Symes & Meadmore have analysed how the school uniform and more generally dress codes and 'various devices of appearance' (1996: 171) 'represent a complex dialectic, formed from a range of clothing discourses … that deal with the moral place of the body in a particular culture, and the positions of bodies within its fabric' (1996: 172). It is in this sense that the school is able to deploy the uniform as a regulatory means to monitor students' appearance and behaviours:

We suggest that the generating scripts underpinning the uniform … connect with more encompassing rationalizing discourses concerned with appearance and the management of the body generally … not always evident as discrete practices, they are connected to a whole system of educational tactics centred on subjectification, on the regulation of the minds and bodies of the school population (1996: 173–74).

What is also significant in the student's words is the way the uniform is described as 'gay'. Thus, we see the way students may emulate and are complicit in maintaining similar and interconnected regulatory practices of normalisation that they are also resisting, of which the uniform is just one example. His homophobic description of the school uniform highlights the panopticonic system of control at work within his school. While feeling watched and regulated, his homophobic reference indicates that he is also one of the watchers and categorisers. Thus, both teachers and students, in relation to uniform and other codes of behaviour and performativity, are implicated within and affected by practices of surveillance and control.

The following boy also highlighted the above oppressed/ oppressor nature of such regulatory practices of surveillance and control at school through his analogy of the 'German concentration camp'. In fact, the idea of school as a Nazi prison camp was reiterated by many students. However, this boy's rejection of the school's legitimation of hierarchical power relations and subjugation of students emerges as a particular instance of enacting a transgressive protest masculinity (Connell, 1995; Walker, 1988) that is complicit in maintaining hegemonic masculinist performativity:

- Life for me at X school is like being held captive in a German concentration camp. Every day is spent trying to escape the reality that we have to dress like poofters and be dominated by overrated teachers with personal problems. It is for this reason that we are known as the school's 'deviants'. Recess and lunch is spent smoking to relieve the stress that is placed upon us. The generalisation 'deviant' and the fact that many people who are unfairly treated are placed under this title makes this group of people special because they are placed under a number of harsh restraints.
Teachers constantly hound us and the benefit of the doubt is unheard of. We are often conspired upon and sting operations are set up to catch us doing something but we are too smart to get caught.
     With the absence of pink (pussy) many are forced to fantasise about undesirable bushpig teachers and if

there was chicks no-one could pull any because we all look like fucking boy scouts.

Being in a private school there are many yuppy wankers who think they are hot shit, however in a school community where only top blokes are accepted most people are frowned upon because of their rich sheltered lives and immature ways they socialise. Social outcasts (anyone who is not accepted by our group) keep out of the way in fear of being harassed. A very real pecking order is in place and to maintain respect people have to apply authority (SSBS 12/17).

The imposition of hierarchical power leads this boy and his peer group to engage in certain rebellious acts through which they are able to establish a particular 'cool' status at the top of the hierarchy of masculinities at this school (see Connell, 1989; Martino & Pallotta-Chiarolli, 2003). Tied to the performance of this kind of rebel masculinity is the act of smoking which he claims is a means of 'relieving stress' created by the school's rigid and 'harsh restraints'. It is quite possible that he is performing this script for us as researchers in an act of defiance against the moral regulation and what appears to be an investment in the fashioning of a particular class-based subjectivity endorsed within that school community. This becomes evident in his reference to 'yuppie wankers who think they are hot shit'. There is a strong sense here of a particular Australian version of hegemonic anti-authoritarian working class masculinity emerging in his discourse with the reference to 'top blokes' who are set against the rich boys who lead 'sheltered lives' (see Martino, 2000). The performance of this masculinity, as it is inscribed in his writing, is manifested through homophobia, sexism and misogyny. This is reflected in his use of language such as 'poofters', 'pussy' and his reference to being 'forced to fantasise' about sex with female 'bushpig' teachers in the absence of girls in this single sex boys' context.

This boy is also quite aware of the collective power of deploying this particular form of ascendant hegemonic heterosexual masculinity at his school, which is enforced through bullying practices directed at the 'social outcasts' – a status which is defined by this dominant group of boys (see Connell, 1987). In this way, they maintain their place at the top of a pecking order of masculinities at school (see Kessler et al., 1985; Mac an Ghaill, 1994; Skelton, 1998). What also needs to be stressed is that this boy demonstrates a particular investment in this practice of masculinity because of the power and status that is accrued to such boys through fashioning themselves in this way. However, ironically, while rejecting the school's imposition of hierarchical power relations, he takes on an identical power structure which he enforces collectively in terms of bullying those students who are deemed to be social outcasts and relegated a position at the bottom of the social hierarchy of masculinities at this school.

Other boys also mentioned and were critical of the classist nature of the school culture which they saw reflected in the behaviour of both their peers and teachers:

- For me school is darn boring. Going to a boys' school full of rich snobby little city kids and old grey beard men stuck in the 20s for teachers. My parents or my old man wastes 8 grand a year sending me to this place that I hate plus my marks are no better than when I went to a government school. But when I went there I liked school a lot more. Normal people and girls and some half decent teachers. At my school the teachers have a sad if you don't say 'yes sir' when answering the roll ... Those teachers think they've got us on a leash but we get up to plenty they don't know about. All the teachers try and catch us but they never score (SSBS 16/16).

- X is a single sex college. There are very strict regulations, classes are very formal and everything 'is done by the book'. The college has a rich tradition which has set the standard for certain activities in the school ... More responsibility should be placed in the hands of the boys, allowing them to develop leadership and people skills ... Tradition plays an important role in the uniform which is very uncomfortable. Long knee-high socks are a thing of the past. Get rid of them (SSBS 19/16).

Both these boys mention the extent to which they feel their school is locked into a 'time warp' where unnecessary traditionalist approaches and methods of relating to students are endorsed. But such practices appear to be tied up with regulatory and moral imperatives of schooling organised around the production of white middle class subjectivities. The call for more responsibility to be placed in the hands of students was frequently reiterated by many of the students in all schools we surveyed. This highlights the extent to which the culture of such schools appeared to be characterised by very traditional and authoritarian approaches to students. This seemed to be related to the issue of repressive student/teacher relations and a reluctance to provide opportunities for students to 'develop wise judgements and to exercise their autonomy in responsible ways' (Collins et al., 2000: 101).

BOYS' SEXUALISED HUMOUR AND BULLYING IN SCHOOLS

A number of boys at the single sex boys' school, such as is evident in the following example, used humour – in a strategic subversive manner – to attempt a disruption of the institutionalised regimes of power and authority invested in the teachers and the 'headmaster'. While we acknowledge once again the performative dimension of this script directed to us as outsiders to the school community and written perhaps to shock us, we are interested in how it represents another instance of boys deploying a form of sardonic homophobic humour to disrupt the middle class power authority structure that is imposed on students, as well as to enact a particular version of masculinity (see Kehily & Nayak, 1997):

- School can be described as the most important part of my life. I don't know what I would do without it. School, to me is the only part of the day that makes me feel alive.
    The teachers at my school are the most original interesting people I have ever been lucky enough to come in contact with. They are fair, bright and all individual, life at school without them would not be worth the time of day. If I was within the law I would make animal love with every one of them.

>   The fact that I only have one year of school left is not something to be happy about. If it were possible I would attend school for at least another 12 years.
>   As for the issues which I face every day. As I am at an all-boys school the temptation to take another boy into the headmaster's office and have numerous sexual pleasures is too great to resist. The only problem here is that this office is always occupied by one boy. His close relationship with the headmaster has become a very important issue throughout the school. As this has become public #### has left our school and moved in with the headmaster. I have taken over #### role with the headmaster and the time has come to pay another visit to him (SSBS 21/16).

While this student appears to be using homophobia and pedophilia to generate a particular humorous response from his reader, other boys in fact highlighted the homophobic bullying and violence that seemed to be endemic at this school:

> - For starters I hate school. I don't like most of the people in my year or school. Mainly because of what I have copped from people. I hate the homophobia that seems to come with a good 90% of the boys. I'm not gay but homophobia fucks me off. I hate fighting, our school is plagued with people who want to fight and it's pathetic. Our school is full of gangs and homies, it makes life really difficult. I hate the order of our school. I want it to be more free flowing and not tied down. When it comes down to it I'm a bit of a punk out of place, but I don't boot in heads and I don't parade myself. The school tries to fit me in but they just grind me against the grain more ... I do a bit of piss and pot, not much pot, just to get away. I'm fine out of school. This place fucks me around (SSBS 5/16).

At this school 37% (26 boys) made some comment about bullying or the compulsion that many boys felt to measure up to their peers' expectations. The above student also draws a significant link between drug/alcohol use and the stresses resulting from an oppressive school culture in which he feels trapped and where bullying and harassment are rife. This highlights the need for schools to take some responsibility for interrogating their role in creating the conditions that produce high levels of stress for some students who may seek escape through drug and alcohol use. This link between school culture and students' risk taking behaviours is not addressed in health education policies where peer group pressure and external societal factors are always given as reasons driving such behaviours.

Such accounts also call into question claims made in a study by Hulse (1997) conducted in the United States. Hulse argues that boys attending single sex schools are advantaged in terms of their emotional, psychological and intellectual development. This study involved comparing boys' motivation, attitude to school and self-esteem at a single sex and co-educational school. On the basis of her research Hulse draws the following conclusions, which are not supported by our surveys and earlier interviews with boys (see Martino & Pallotta-Chiarolli, 2003). She states that boys from boys' schools:

- are less defensive and less susceptible to social pressures than the boys who attend co-ed school;
- may feel that they have more options available to them as they define their masculinity;
- have a higher sense of control over their performance than co-ed school boys;
- are less in conflict about aspects of their environment than are boys who attend co-educational schools;
- feel more comfortable about their relationship with girls than do boys who attend a co-ed school;
- have more egalitarian attitudes towards women's and men's roles in society than do the boys who attend co-educational schools (1997: 18).

The further claims that 'boys' school boys seem better able to retain their independence from peer group pressures' are not supported by the boys in our study who, like the above students, highlighted the impact of a pecking order of masculinities on their lives in the single sex school context (see also White, 2004). Furthermore, disturbing claims that 'boys' school boys feel the school protects them and allows them appropriately to express their aggression' (1997: 18) require some critical examination, given the essentialising and naturalising tendencies implicated in such discourses about masculinity (see Petersen, 2000). This perspective is informed by a discourse which claims that boys are naturally disposed to expressing aggressive behaviours and that an all-boys environment enables boys to do this *appropriately* without the requirement they might feel to repress such behaviour due to the presence of girls:

> Maybe Cory feels he can never look quite attractive enough for girls and maybe he would like to be more rough and tumble but has to control himself in front of girls (Hulse, 1997: 11).

What is not mentioned at all in the study, which relies on psychological testing scales for measuring attitude and motivation, is the pervasive role of bullying and sex-based harassment that governs the fashioning of normative hegemonic heterosexual masculinity in school contexts, both single sex and co-educational (see Frank, 1987, 1993; Mac an Ghaill, 1994, 2000; Collins et al., 1996; Laskey & Beavis, 1996; Epstein & Johnson, 1998; Epstein et al., 1998; Walker, 1988; Davison, 2000; Martino, 2000; Renold, 2001a). In fact, Robinson argues that such harassment in schools is denied and trivialised 'under the veil of male normality, thus largely rendering the behaviour invisible' (2000: 76). Moreover, she claims that a particular aggressive and coercive approach to discipline practices in the single sex boys' school in her study 'reflected philosophies and practices perpetuating hegemonic masculinity' (2000: 78). Such research indicates that further investigation is required into the impact of school cultures on students' relations and an exploration of how bullying and sex-based harassment is being addressed in schools. As Collins et al. claim, further research is needed which addresses:

> The whole pattern of sex-based harassment in schools; who the harassers are and how sex-based harassment fits into broader power games among boys and relates to the construction of gender in girls as a group (1996: 179).

PERFORMING HETEROSEXUAL MASCULINITY

Indeed, the student narratives from the co-educational schools in our survey supported the above contention that some boys' performances of hegemonic heterosexuality and misogyny, as displayed in the research process, were normalised in co-educational settings as well, and that both other boys and girls, including female teachers, were the recipients and targets of such performances of dominant masculinity. Thus, rather than boys feeling they have to control their 'rough and tumble' behaviours in front of girls, as Hulse (1997) suggests, girls become convenient points of reference and targets in the exacerbation of the performance of a misogynist heterosexual masculinity:

- Boys are sexually frustrated at school. Teachers pick on me because I'm sexy (GHSV M 128/16).

- The world's against boys in schools, especially hot guys like me. I fantasise about raping people, so great is my sexual frustration (GHSV M 130/16).

- Problems I have at school are teachers on their rags and teachers who haven't had sex in years (GHSV M 207/16).

What is also of interest is how several boys in co-educational settings also constructed girls' experiences at school as a point of comparison to their own experiences and stated that boys' experiences were much more positive:

- I don't have to deal with any issues because I'm a boy (GHSV M 24/16).

However, the presence of girls was often blamed for distracting boys from their study, in line with Hulse's (1997) comments and the view often endorsed by educational policy advocating single sex groupings for boys (see Martino et al., 2004). However, what is absent in these debates and Hulse's discussion is the social construction of a dominant masculinity that endorses and demands that boys assert dominance over and engage sexually with girls as a prime definer and proof of their 'normality' as heterosexual boys:

- Boys have it bloody easy at school. Boys have no issues, except for when you can't get a girlfriend (GHSV M 210/16).

- I feel pressured to communicate with the opposite sex as there are many people who do this. This makes me depressed when I can't communicate and disturbs my concentration and work attitudes (GHSV M 164/16).

Yet, as research shows, these boys' supposed 'distraction' from learning due to the presence of girls is no different to the 'distraction' from learning that boys claim to experience in single sex schools due to the absence of girls. In each case, the issue is having to conform to the dictates of compulsory heterosexuality which require a public performance of a masculinity that is organised around the sexual objectification of girls.

The following boys' comments throw into question Hulse's claims that the single sex school is more conducive to boys' healthy expression of masculinity and 'appropriate aggression'. For some boys, the absence of girls accounts for the high incidence of bullying at the school:

- ... the most frustrating thing is the lack of women ... I suppose that's why there's so much bullying in our school. In conclusion this school sux ARS!!! (SSBS 30/16).

In the following, while mentioning 'the freedom to do and say what [he] likes with no girls around', this student notes that many boys go too far in terms of disrupting classes, which is the very behaviour that feminist educators have indicated impacts detrimentally on girls in co-educational schools (see Spender, 1982; Younger & Warrington, 1996; Rennie & Parker, 1997; Lee, 1998; Mahony, 1998; Younger et al., 1999; Francis, 2000; Jackson & Smith, 2000):

- I like being at an all-guy school, I think it provides us with the freedom to do and say what we like with no girls around making us worry about image and stuff. Freedom to act exactly as we wish without worrying

> about image is something I like. But some guys need to have a bit of restriction as they can go too far and the level of disruption in our classes, whilst fun, is too high. In an all-male environment it is also my fear that we are harbouring another generation of men stuck in social stereotypes of 'real men' that should have been extinct 30 years ago. General attitudes on women and academic success and drugs etc are being bred in our school that is nothing short of disturbing. Compulsory sport, while I love it, it is not for everyone and I know a lot of people who have a lot of trouble dealing with this. I think that the disruption in classes has a direct effect on our learning as 15 minutes of the hour is spent teaching, the other 45 disciplining people. There is also a lot of drugs being taken at our school, I observe that peer pressure has had a grave effect on many people's lives, many very smart people have chosen a different direction for their life with their friends and wasted all their potential. Example, one boy came in Year 8 – he was quite smart but very shy – was made miserable for 2 years, did a lot of drugs. 6 months ago he died of a heroin overdose (SSBS 36/16).

This kind of behaviour is also rejected by and impacts on those boys at this school who are committed to their studies. SSBS 36 also seems to provide evidence to refute the claim that boys' schools cultivate 'more egalitarian attitudes towards women's and men's roles in society' (Hulse, 1997: 18) with his comments about the general attitudes 'being bred' about women, academic success and drugs which, he claims, are 'nothing short of disturbing'. His reference to the influence of peer pressure also challenges Hulse's assertion that 'boys seem better able to retain their independence from peer group pressure' (1997: 18). He even provides the example of the tragic death of a boy from his school who died of a heroin overdose, which he links to such practices of peer group pressure.

In fact, one boy mentions that school 'isn't too bad' but qualifies his assertion by mentioning that he is 'part of the crowd' and, hence, not an outcast:

> • School isn't too bad because I am part of the crowd. In the early years of senior school, anyone who wasn't part of the crowd was isolated and teased (i.e. too smart, too dumb, too fat, too thin, etc) ... (SSBS 29/15).

In the light of the above discussions by boys and researchers such as Hulse (1997) in regard to the superiority of single sex settings for boys and the 'problem' of girls being a distracting presence in co-educational schools, it is interesting to see how many girls in the single sex girls' school, in discussing the advantages of being in their school, turned the gaze back onto boys' single-sex schooling environments and what they perceived to be its limitations:

> • Being a girl at school is good in some ways but these ways only become obvious when you see what boys go through. Boys are treated impersonally, called by their last names as if they are always doing something wrong. They also get bashed up, and it's normal for them, and are 'sissies' if they tell. At an all-girls school if you so much as lay a finger on someone else they are in big trouble. Astronomical trouble. Suspension even (SSGS 25/15).
>
> • I hardly see boys' schools studying books like we do and some of the health issues we deal with [in our studies] (SSGS 164/16).

Many of these young women also contrasted the advantages for girls in single sex schools to the disadvantages girls in co-educational schools experienced due to the presence and predominance of boys. Thus, their reasons for attending a single sex school were directly and strongly linked to the gender-based hierarchies and harassment they considered to be a 'normal' part of co-educational schools:

> • It's good cos you don't have to look good every day for boys (SSGS 65/15).
>
> • At a girls' school issues such as periods and other things are freely discussed and aren't laughed at by anybody (SSGS 86/15).

- We don't get intimidated or distracted by boys in class and we seem to all get along and work together ... there tends to not be any physical fighting as there might be with boys (SSGS 116/16).

- At co-ed schools girls have pressure to laugh along at the boys. The boys show off and I think girls must fill a role. It's too macho, that's why I prefer a single sex school (SSGS 160/15).

SINGLE SEX OR CO-EDUCATIONAL SCHOOLING FOR BOYS

In light of what the above girls say about the pervasive nature of gendered social hierarchies in co-educational schools, it is significant that boys from co-educational schools also wrote about harassment perpetrated by dominant 'cool' boys and foregrounded the pressure involved in conforming to peer group norms. In addition, the following boy asserts that teachers are implicated in perpetrating a particular power dynamic in their relationship with boys that is not dissimilar to that perpetrated by bullies. He draws attention to how even the bullies feel the need to prove and situate themselves within a hierarchy of masculinities:

- The teachers are absolute control freaks. Some of them feel they need to pick on students as examples to others. They often focus on some intellectual students and forget about the rest ... As a boy I feel there is more pressure placed on you by other members of the same sex to conform to their ideas and if you don't you shall be harassed both physically and mentally. I experience problems but so does everyone else. Even those who make other people's problems – i.e. bullies, because they feel they need to prove themselves (CCHS M 34/15).

Other boys from the Catholic co-educational school also commented on the abusive power of teachers:

- School sucks and I think the teachers are up themselves and powerfreaks ... Boys have to put up with macho dickhead teachers who think they rule the school (CCHS M 40/16).

- Most teachers are shit boring and I'd rather watch my dog lick its own balls (CCHS M 66/15).

Many boys from the suburban co-educational government school in Perth even compared their school to a prison, highlighting the extent to which they felt restricted and subjugated:

- They put up a barbwire fence that goes all around the school like a fucking prison. It's more or less like a Catholic school now, and it's getting worse. I'm holding my girlfriend's hand or hugging her or whatever and a teacher would walk past and say 'split up, not at school please'. I mean c'mon, it's recess and lunch, our break from school work and you can't even spend time with your girlfriend. It's bullshit (GHS M 202/15).

This boy also draws on a populist discourse about private versus public education to reiterate the more restricted and regimented disciplining of students associated with private schooling (Wilkinson et al., 2004). In fact, some boys differentiated between the standard of education in government and private schools. They believed private school settings afforded shelter from harsher realities and were better resourced:

- School is there to provide education that is of a poor standard. Every day I turn up to the same boring classes and we have to work in appalling conditions ... being a boy has nothing to do with anything, everyone is treated the same and if you can't deal with the issues and put up with the pressure you should be in a private school (GHSVM 28/16).

However, boys in both suburban and rural co-educational government schools were critical of the way discipline problems were handled and mentioned that nothing was done to address bullying in school:

- Sometimes school really sux because there are too many bullies and the teachers do nothing about it sometimes (GHS M/ 21 /14).

- About the only problem I have with school is when teachers don't believe me. Like recently I was suspended for something I didn't do. I tried and I tried explaining to the principal that I didn't do anything. But she took the other kid's (the kid that I was supposed to have hurt) word over mine and it wasn't until I got my parents up to talk to the principal that she actually listened to what I had to say. That is about my only problem at school that teachers don't listen to what I have to say enough (RGHS M 12/16).

However, one boy indicated that students did abuse and threaten teachers:

- The M.S.B. [Managing Student Behaviour] department isn't managed well either, kids swear at teachers, threaten them and they're in the classroom the next day (GHS M 219/15).

CONCLUSION

On the basis of what many boys had to say about their experience of schooling, most of the schools seemed to be characterised by a culture of repressive student/teacher relations and a hyper-rationalist focus on controlling and disciplining students (see Kenway et al., 1997). This, coupled with the effects of a hierarchical pecking order of peer group social relations, led many students to construct life at school as an unbearable experience. The following student brings all these issues together as he moves from a focus on the particular culture of sport that is endorsed officially at his school to a discussion of the impact and effect of masculinity on his life:

- School is crap. The teachers drive me up the wall. Mainly because they hold grudges and don't forgive for previous mistakes. They accuse and abuse me. They only honour sporting achievements and continuously make reference to these. They prefer to bury you than to look for your talent. This is generalising though, the teachers that treat you like a human get respect ... Being a boy at school is two sided, the teachers automatically take a disliking to me because I'm not gifted academically or athletically and because I can be a smart arse. Being a boy at school worries me because it means that you have to be emotionally strong and not get upset. You also have to be physically strong or sexually experienced or you will face rejection from fellow classmates. These are the issues males deal with because of the way our gender has developed. There is also pressure on us to mature faster and to develop into 'real men' or 'get our act together' (CCHS M 9/16).

The above boy highlights how the culture both cultivated and legitimated by a particular school can be alienating to certain students who do not fit neatly into the proscribed categories of success invested either in sporting achievement or academic performance (see White, 2004). This is exacerbated by the anxiety that is induced as a result of feeling compelled to live up to the dictates of a hegemonic heterosexual 'cool' masculinity which involve being physically strong and sexually experienced in order to gain acceptance from his peers. Both these issues relating to the culture of schools and peer group relations also emerged, as will be discussed in the next chapter, as significant in how the girls constructed their experiences of schooling.

BOYS AND SCHOOL

AIM • To develop a deeper understanding about boys' experiences of school structures and culture

AUTHORITARIAN POWER

As teachers, we need to distinguish between authoritarian and authoritative uses of power in schools. Using top-down approaches to discipline and behaviour management can often exacerbate and incite boys' resistance to schooling.

FOR REFLECTION

- How might teachers and school principals enhance more autonomy and self-regulation without having to resort to enforcing hierarchical, top-down forms of power?
- What kinds of power relations are modelled at school for students? Is power imposed or negotiated?

SCHOOL CULTURE

As a school, we need to create less repressive and oppressive school structures. This involves including students in the development and negotiation of school-based rules and regulations.

FOR REFLECTION

- Rather than rigidly enforcing rules, how can schools encourage boys to take more responsibility for their own learning and behaviour at school?
- What kind of student/teacher relationships would foster building such a school culture?

SEXUALISED BULLYING

We need to depoliticise bullying and to understand its sexualised dimensions. Boys tend to use homophobia and sexuality to engage in a form of male humour. This kind of behaviour is trivialised and is not addressed in schools and is often related to compulsory heterosexuality and the failure of schools to address more broadly the impact of heterosexism.

BOYS AND SCHOOL   49

FOR REFLECTION
- How might all teachers start to critically examine homophobia, heterosexism and compulsory heterosexuality in schools?
- What role do these play in creating a particular school culture?

DISCUSSION FORUM

Select a group of student writings and discuss the following questions:
- Identify the issues related to gender, school culture and learning that the students raise about their experiences of school.
- To what extent do current policies in your school pay heed to or take into account the issues raised by these students?
- What strategies could be adopted in the classroom to facilitate a dialogue with students about effective and productive schooling?

GROUP 1

- School sucks, get up early, do boring work, get yelled at, deal with crap teachers, spend 13 years of our lives doing something totally boring (GHSV M 207/16).

- Being a boy I feel pressured to get myself a girlfriend. This sometimes interferes with my homework as I am constantly distracted by my thoughts of women (GHSV M 166/16).

- For me school is educational, a place to meet with your friends and play sport. Being a boy at school is easy, just be yourself ... (GHSV M 88/16).

- School is like a meeting place for friends, which also offers us an education. Being a boy at school is quite relaxing and enjoyable. The only trouble I have is dealing with the workload (GHSV M 10/16).

GROUP 2

- Girls in co-ed schools have a much more negative attitude and are very defensive when conflicts arise. In girls-only schools, they are much nicer and open to accept others. I have come to realise that my duration at a co-ed school was simply seen as 'being there'. I was not as welcomed as I was at the girls' school. At a co-ed school, I simply existed without much meaning, but attending a girls' school was much more enjoyable (SSGS 122/16).

- I feel it is best for me that I am at a girls' school. Specially I am not as pretty or as attractive as some of the other girls and sometimes when boys come into the situations it is very noticeable ... I have also noticed how immature some of the boys can be also just the way they talk and address people (SSGS 155/16).

GROUP 3

- School is just like society except it's smaller and you learn more. We have the people in charge (teachers), the people who represent the main body of our mini-society (the student representative council), and we have students as the main body. We have a social order, the popular people and the social outcasts, people who make you feel good and people who just want to step on you. All of this goes on as we learn. To most people life revolves around learning. Most conversations start with 'What have you got next?' But even so, most people and me especially, like to forget about what we did in maths or science that day (the only time we'll use it again is in our next test). Some people forget by going out, some with drugs, some just think about it. For me, release from school is sport ... Some people think that life in school is made miserable by teachers. It's not, but they help. Good days usually change into bad days during lunch or recess. Someone says this, someone says that ...

someone doesn't say what you want them to. Actual school work really only adds pressure. Assignments just mean getting 4 hrs sleep the night before it's due. Homework is something I do in the homeroom before 1st period starts. School life is meant to revolve around learning. It doesn't. As far as I can see it revolves around the social life of students. Learning is just something we do on the side (CCHS M 29/15).

GROUP 4

- The only problems I experience at school are some of the teachers' inability to hear or even understand a concept or idea that is not one of their own (CCHS M 52/16).

- The school that I'm at was once a good school with no uniform, no 6 foot high fence with 4 rings of barbed wire around it which basically turned the school into a prison. When you go past the school you would think that it was a detention centre. As for the uniform, which is plain blue, it sucks … Most of the teachers in the school try to play God with you. All the teachers have walkie-talkies, what next? Also, every time you are suspected of something they just search your bag, which I see as an invasion of privacy (GHS M 268/16).

- The way this school handles behaviour is ridiculous. They don't even listen to you, they just suspend you straight away. So my behaviour would be my only problem at school and also probably not doing my work but I can't help that (GHS M 214/16).

- Many teachers are unfair and never listen to what you have to say, when you are in trouble and when you do say something they call it back-chatting (GHS M 227/15).

2

GIRLS AND SCHOOL
'School is a pain in the butt'

• There's too much pressure, pressure to get a good mark, a good ENTER score, into the right university. You have to be strong or it'll wear you away, eat at you. Competition, competition, competition, and our school really pushes the competitive streak, it's a race, have no social life, no free time, focus on your school work ... our society puts too much emphasis on academia. Life would be much worse I think if we ... were all able to recite the elements, electronegativity, shell configuration and subshell configuration of every element on the periodic table. We have RE [religious education] time and I wish in this time we could focus more on becoming good people ... why can't we spend more time improving society, so many just don't care (SSGS 157/16).

IN THIS CHAPTER YOU WILL:

• learn more about what girls really think about school teachers;

• develop a greater understanding about female resistance to teachers and school-based authority;

• learn more about the impact of social hierarchies on girls' experiences of schooling;

• engage in a Professional Development session using girls' voices to build knowledge about effective schooling for girls.

INTRODUCTION

In this chapter, we explore how a diverse range of girls in different schools view education and learning. Despite backlash educational constructions of 'girls have it easy at school', we found that girls expressed similar views to boys about school and teachers, often drawing attention to the uses and abuses of power within school structures and by teachers. This is very significant in light of the literature which has tended to highlight boys' resistance to schooling and institutional authority in schools that is often manifested as a form of protest masculinity (see Willis, 1977; Walker, 1988; Connell, 1989).

FEMALE RESISTANCE TO TEACHERS AND SCHOOL-BASED AUTHORITY

The following students' responses were fairly representative of the girls' resistance to teachers and school-based authority:

- People think that girls have mood swings, but have they met the teachers! It's ridiculous how much their personality changes through a lesson (SSGS 111/15).

- We need more independence. Constantly we are yelled at and spoken to like babies (SSGS 69/15).

Given the debates on the need for more male teachers for male students, it is interesting that some young women pointed out the limitations of male teachers in relation to the gendered concerns of female students:

- Male teachers have a different response to us compared to the female ones because they don't know the hardships of being female (SSGS 71/15).

- One teacher used to favour guys over girls but he was an idiot and not a good reflection of the other teachers here (GHSV F 219/16).

In her research, Francis explored students' perceptions of boys' laddish behaviour in school, which rests on a narrative about female passivity and male activity as binary oppositional gendered behaviours. Francis claims that 'the classroom observation did suggest that boys tended to be louder and more demanding than girls and use more physical forms of resistance in the classroom' (2000: 115). This relates to the issue of boys' overt and active resistance to schooling being set against girls' passive conformity and just sitting quietly. However, Francis does highlight the need to attend to the contradictions in young people's talk about their experiences of schooling and claims that 'some people consistently maintained in their interviews that there is little or no difference in male and female classroom behaviour' (2000: 113).

Our research tends to support this with regards to the issue of student resistance to teachers and school-based power structures. We contend that the girls' rejection and critical appraisal of schooling, documented below, may be articulated in more tacit ways at school and not necessarily through the overt bodily enactment of disrupting classes and 'mucking around' that characterises boys' performance of protest masculinities (see Gilbert & Gilbert, 1998; Martino, 2001).

- School for me is hard, boring and something I pretty much hate ... I wish I didn't go to school, I just like hanging out at train stations with my cousin drinking all day. It's so easy to wag, and what's the point in going when the teachers tell you to cut off your orange dreadlocks! It's a fashion statement! (SSGS 111/15).

While some girls adopt overt strategies of resistance exemplified by the above student, others talk about consciously performing a traditional and compliant femininity in order to make life at school easier:

- What really gets me through school is the 'smile and nod' manoeuvre – be polite and others will more likely go out of their way to help you (SSGS 1/15).

- The teachers are dickheads who have no idea what they are on about. Being a girl is easier though because

if you just bat your eyes and start to cry none of the
men teachers can do anything to you (CCHS F 127/15).

CCHS 127 emphasises that it is 'easier' for girls, in one sense, because they can use their sexuality and dominant constructs of a sexualised and emotionally sensitive femininity to manipulate male teachers.

Overall, the following comments were representative of the girls' perspectives on schooling. They tended to construct school and specifically teachers in terms that paralleled the boys' perspectives:

- School for me is a pain in the butt. I hate it. It can be fun sometimes but most of the time it's a bunch of loser teachers pushing you around because they like the power (GHS F 92/15).

- I don't think teachers at my school really act like they enjoy teaching and it makes it a drag to come to school and listen to people who don't want to be there anyway. They don't seem interested in the students as people at all ... are uninspiring and look like they are grumpy all the time. They don't reward us for doing things well but they punish us for doing things bad (SSGS 23/15).

Like the boys, the girls also deployed the metaphor of the prison to capture their sentiments about schooling:

- I think it's pretty weird that we're stuck in school for 13 years straight and murderers and rapists so often get just a few years ... (SSGS 32/15).

- Our school has fences 6 foot high with barbed wire on top with whopping big padlocks that are locked 8.30 am till 3 pm so no-one can get out and no-one can get in. School is way out of control. People do and say what they like and also take what they want too ... Girls have it the same as boys. We both get suspended, we both get yelled at by teachers and we both get shit! (GHS F 93/15).

- I feel that I don't get any excitement out of school. It makes me feel like we are in a prison and constantly nagged with new school rules. I've thought about it and I've realised we need our education to get somewhere in life but why are teachers so demanding? Sometimes being a girl, I feel there is a lot of discrimination towards us. Teachers may sometimes take things the wrong way, so we are never heard out (GHS F 122/15).

While school is constructed as a prison sentence for these girls, the issue appears to be one related to their treatment at the hands of teachers who are represented as oppressive and inflexible in their approach to dealing with students. Thus as GHS 122 explains, the concern is less about the significance of education per se and more to do with its delivery and the nature of the social and pedagogical interaction between students and teachers (see Ancess, 2003; see Lingard, B, Martino, W, Mills, M & Bahr, M, 2003).

In the following, CCHS 111 suggests that the gendered expectations of teachers with regards to girls sitting quietly accounts for greater surveillance and monitoring of their overtly resistant behaviour. Since this behaviour is not expected of boys, this student appears to be saying that they can get away with talking and inattentive behaviour whereas girls cannot because it defies constructs of passive, acceptable femininity (Lee 1998; Harris, 1999; 2004):

- Being a girl, sitting quietly in class is a hard task. We constantly get into trouble for talking whilst the boys chat happily away. At the end of the class when the teacher sees the boys' work isn't done the whole class is punished even if some did do the set work! Asking to go to the toilet is like trying to immigrate to another country sometimes. It's not like we are going to raid the office supplies or anything. These make things hard for girls at particular times of the month. Too much pressure is placed on us to succeed but how can we when we don't enjoy being there. I've got heaps more to say, but I can't be stuffed! (CCHS F 111/15).

Thus, many girls reject the gendered nature of the policing of their femininities through restrictive school rules, as well as the regulatory systems that problematise bodily functions such as menstruation: 'at particular times of the month'. As Harris writes,

> bodies cannot be neatly split off from the social world within which they are experienced, used, disciplined and represented ... the meanings attached to [female] adolescence, as a bodily process, are deeply embedded in the sociocultural space of patriarchy (1999: 112; see also Lee 1998; Diorio & Munro, 2000; Kehily et al., 2002; Tanenbaum 2002; Harris, 2004).

This raises the point reiterated by many students regarding the social and gendered dimensions of peer group relations and hierarchies, which proved to be a major issue for the girls as well.

SOCIAL HIERARCHIES FOR GIRLS AT SCHOOL

The following girls highlight the issue of multiple femininities and social hierarchies amongst girls, which is erased in the public debates about boys' education. They also draw the link between social class, one's positioning in the peer group hierarchy at school and the implications of this for their engagement with learning:

- School to me is a very social place. School is also 'the' place for social class rating. People at my school are classed into groups according to gender, personality, intelligence, how they look and how they dress. High school is very hard and tough as far as social classes go. Depending on what 'group' you are in depends on how many friends you have, how you are treated and how accepted you are by other peers ... Being a girl at school is very hard. Girls are the worst for social acceptance. To be in 'the popular group' you have to be very social, good-looking, wear name brand and the 'in' clothes, be able to do basically whatever you want, i.e., go to parties, stay out late, etc ... The problems I experience at school are social acceptance. I am in the 'popular'

group at school and have high expectations in which to
stay in that group (GHS F 115/15).

- You are either wealthy or incredibly smart. I am
neither so the feeling of being an outcast often
emerges. While we get a first-rate education I find
myself spending more time worrying about what girls
will think of me rather than studying and that bothers
me (SSGS 143/16).

- I think being at an all-girls school is just like a big
popularity contest. Everyone is trying to be better,
look better and act better than everyone else.
Sometimes this gets in the way of people's learning at
school and I think that's really sad, because basically
all we want to do is get smarter in a nice environment
(SSGS 49/15).

Teachers may also be implicated in perpetuating social hierarchies of femininity organised around the norm of the passive, disciplined and compliant student. The following girl draws attention to how a certain 'type of girl' may get constructed by teachers as 'perfect', given greater opportunities and placed on a pedestal as a leader:

- I think boys are able to express themselves more
while girls are expected to conform ... At the same
time I think girls have more opportunities and are able
to find themselves more at a girls' school ... although I
think that some of them are limited to a certain type
of girl that appeals to teachers; studious, dedicated,
disciplined, etc when really girls who aren't perfect
should be given opportunities, especially to lead. After
all, what good is a perfect leader if it means they can't
relate to the majority who aren't? (SSGS 109/16).

The intersections between gendered and racialised hierarchies were also pointed out by some girls. This is evident in the way the following girl draws attention to the intra-hierarchies of femininity-based on an inferiorisation of 'being an Asian', which intersects with a particular gender system whereby 'immature' boys are constructed as impeding girls' learning in school.

> • Girls are quickly categorised and once you are it's hard to remove that label from yourself. I'm thankful though that I'm Australian because it would suck being an Asian because they get so much shit! ... I also think that being a girl in lower school it's harder with the boys because they're so immature it affects us who want to concentrate and excel. Overall personally I think being a girl in a Catholic school is hard and trying to live up to expectations is even harder (CCHS F 86/16).

One girl even indicated that, contrary to dominant discourses that achieving at school is not considered 'cool' by boys, this may also apply and contribute to perpetuating social hierarchies amongst girls. Being 'cool' for girls also involves a particular regulated social behaviour and policing that includes going to parties, drinking, and having a social life. However, what she foregrounds is the heightened significance of appearance, body image and weight for girls in order to gain a particular status within the gendered social hierarchies in school. Overlaying these social hierarchies is the very specific role of the structural and cultural hierarchies of the school which celebrate and reward those students who are considered to be 'very sport focused'. While the emphasis in most literature has been on the role sport plays in the fashioning of a 'cool' hegemonic heterosexual masculinity, attention needs to be drawn to the implications of similar social practices for girls.

> • In primary school if you were smart and got good marks everyone thought you were great, but in high school if you are smart everyone thinks you're a squid and uncool etc. At our school there is a major popularity problem with people feeling inferior to the 'cool' group who get that name by being the group that parties, drinks, goes out with each other etc. Majority are good-looking/attractive. This is a problem as others

have self-esteem probs and don't want to ask people they feel are their social level as they might be a try-hard and get less popular. Lots 'suck up' to them to try and get in and feel accepted and betray real friends, If u socialise with those lower u are looked down on. Being a girl u always feel conscious about weight, appearance etc when you have guys and judgmental females who are naturally pretty around all day. These girls get automatically popular through their looks and personality. Also if u aren't good at PE people think you are unco-ordinated and daggy as our school is very sport focused with constant assemblies recognising athletes (CCHS F 91/15).

The only school where many girls were publicly affirming of education and proud of their academic achievements was the single sex school. As SSGS 166 points out in the following, academic achievement and participation in the curriculum is policed through homophobia and femiphobia for boys in ways that limit their choices:

- I think it is easier to be smart if you're a girl because you aren't labelled a nerd, but people actually admire you and envy you ... It is also easier for girls to be musical than boys because we aren't branded geeks or gay, as many boys who sing or play can be (SSGS 166/16).

- I like going to a girls' school because not only does it give us a well-rounded education but we get taught life skills and lessons as well. Our school offers many opportunities in many different fields such as sport, music, drama and languages. Our school has a policy against bullying which is quite effective (SSGS 66/14).

It is interesting how SSGS 66 seems to associate an effective policy against bullying with being provided with a 'well-rounded education' that involves the teaching of particular 'life skills' and also relates to the 'many opportunities' that the school offers for participating in a range of activities and cultural pursuits considered relevant by girls to their everyday lives. However, for some girls, their academic abilities meant they felt superior to other students and could use them as forms of harassment:

- I do love getting pieces of work back and showing off my A+s to everyone and getting them jealous (SSGS 110/16).

Other girls at this school experienced intimidation if they felt unable to measure up academically to the 'smart' girls:

- I do enjoy school but my lack of confidence does affect me, sometimes I am too scared to answer a question in class simply because I am scared girls will laugh or say something if it is wrong (SSGS 138/16).

Girls at the co-educational middle class school, however, found that like boys, they were:

- ... picked on if you're smart. You get called a nerd etc. Other girls think they are the best (the popular ones), put you down because you're not like them (GHSV F 93/16).

For those girls in co-educational schools who wanted to achieve, the behaviour of boys was often presented as not only detrimental to girls' learning but as costing them entry into university:

- Attending a co-ed school has its disadvantages. I find many boys frequently misbehave and are immature, especially around their peers. I wish I attended a single sex school. Boys can be especially disruptive sometimes. They might just cost me my university place ... I strongly believe the state school system education is declining in standard exponentially and wished I was in a single sex school (GHSV F 169/15).

The above student also raises the issue of declining standards in public education, which leads her to express a desire to attend a single sex school. However, what needs to be asked, and which is not being addressed in current debates about the funding and academic standards of private and public schooling, is: to what extent is learning in school impeded by the hegemonic masculine performances and behaviours of dominant boys to the detriment of girls and marginalised boys positioned lower in the social hierarchy? (Epstein et al., 1998; Jackson, 1998).

Because of the intense pressure placed on girls to fit into the 'cool' group, as well as their sexist positioning within intra-hierarchical peer group social relations, the following student claims there should be more of a focus on social welfare issues related to addressing the well-being and care of students (Ancess, 2003). Instead, she indicates that there is more of an investment in what appears to be a petty obsession with students' attempts to violate the school rules concerning uniform and appearance:

- As a student, the way teachers fly around school, and give detentions to students who are wearing 2 rings or 2 pairs of earrings or that their shirts are not tucked in, there is no freedom. Of course if we have strict regulations, we ARE going to rebel. They should be worrying about the drug problems and other harmful situations rather than worrying about if our hair is tied up or not (CCHS F 94 /14).

This need for attention to be directed to the social welfare of students was reiterated by the following girl. Again, we see the call for greater concern with the health and well-being of female students:

- I think school should be more of a time to develop social skills and attitudes so that people could gain a more pragmatic approach to life. Lots of my peers are socially inept and unable to feel compassion towards anyone else. Philosophical, psychological and sociological matters should have greater influence on the curriculum. People can develop their mathematical abilities but personally, many of the people in my year are a mess ... Many of my peers get bad stress, depression, sleeplessness etc over school problems which are not addressed, like study etc (CCHS 110/16).

MENSTRUATION

What is also significant is the attention some girls give to teachers and school structures as causing menstrual concerns, an issue that is not addressed as often as is boys' harassment of girls in relation to menstruation:

> • Being a girl at school is kind of embarrassing because if we have our period we will ask the teacher if we can go to the toilet and the teachers think we are going for a smoke or session in the toilets (GHS F 106/15).

The tendency for teachers to doubt girls' requests concerning the need to genuinely go to the toilet is produced within a culture that subscribes to hierarchical and traditional disciplinary power relations between teachers and students that can be hyper-rationalist and repressive (Collins et al., 2000).

> • When a girl asks to go to the toilet for 'personal reasons' the teachers get highly suspicious to whether you really do have personal problems or just want to nick off for a smoke. Understandable, but I remember a time when I was blessed with the monthly curse during one class, but instead of granting me the toilet pass, I was taken outside by my teacher and given a lecture on smoking in the toilets in class. Now I hadn't smoked a single cigarette and the teacher knew it. So I would appreciate if the teachers would be a little more caring to us girls and not use the expression, 'but it was lunch only 5 minutes ago' (GHS F 20/16).

However, the language of GHS 20 also illustrates the dominant cultural discourse that girls have already internalised, such as menstrual periods being referred to as a 'monthly curse'. This construct is then further affirmed and accentuated by restrictive and problematic school structures, such as the need to obtain toilet passes in the public setting of a classroom, and adult assumptions about normative adolescent behaviour that frame girls' experiences and care of their menstrual periods.

The only school where girls specifically drew attention to how being at that school made it easier to handle their menstrual periods were girls from the single sex girls' school:

- I've noticed we're a lot more open about periods and painful experiences that come with it (SSGS 62/15).

- It's great that you can relate to the emotions and feelings of a majority of people because they all experience practically the same problems as you do. For example, when it is 'that time of the month' when a girl gets her period and she's all cranky and tired and a little bit flustered, every other girl who has her period is able to understand why this girl is acting this way because they experience it too. This sort of understanding for others is important when you are at school (SSGS 127/16).

'FITTING IN'

In the following, CCHS 156 highlights that the problems at school may often relate to social relationships with peers and pressures to conform, to be 'cool', but claims that she does not have to deal with such issues due to the fact that she is accepted by her peers:

- It's not so much the work and study part of things that people have problems over. But more now than I have ever noticed before in previous years of schooling ... people now seem to have problems socially. But lucky for me, I was accepted into a group that has a good amount of great people both girls and boys (CCHS F 156/15).

These issues of 'fitting in' and being accepted by peers were also mentioned by the following students and acknowledged as contributing significantly to the quality of school life:

- High school is easier if you have friends, and if you don't care what people think about you! ... If you were teased at school it probably would be really horrible but school, bully-wise, is fine for me so I don't dread coming. It's harder at school if you're different because there's always someone who'll pick on the difference ... (GHS F 1/15).

- Being a girl at school is pretty hard. Well we don't know what it's like for the boys exactly, but they don't have to deal with periods for one thing and being a girl you're expected to be more than you are. Going through puberty at school is hard too because most boys only look for one thing at our school and if you don't have big breasts they won't even look at you, which can feel pretty bad. I think that girls have very different issues to deal with than boys because I feel, in my group, that if I wear my hair different or wear different clothes to everyone else, I get laughed at and know that people are talking about me behind my back (GHS F 116/15).

- One problem I see is that girls are more supportive for a friend who's having a bad time/problems and guys just don't show any emotion at all, but this is a problem no matter where you are but the 'macho' male is really getting old ... Some kids are constantly picked on their entire life by people who think they are better than them, which is one thing I despise. I hate the hierarchy of high schools (CCHS F 189/15.

The above girls point out three common themes in the way many girls described life at school:
- the existence of social hierarchies within groups of girls;
- the objectification of girls by boys; and
- the surveillance and regulation of girls by boys and other girls based on body image and 'cool' or 'proper' heterosexualised femininity.

These three themes are linked to what Harris defines as 'three kinds of responsibility and containment' that are indicative of a 'successful passage ... to a female maturity', as constructed, defined and policed by patriarchy:

> the first kind involves responsibility for and concealment of the body ... through covering up, concealing 'leaks', and being as physically attractive as possible. The second is sexuality. This includes responsibility for sexual behaviour and 'correct' sexual identity and containment of sexuality ... The third kind is related to emotional responsibility, expressed by being concerned for others and managing emotional relationships, and containing 'inappropriate' emotions (1999: 114; see also Kehily et al., 2002).

GENDERED CONSTRUCTS OF SCHOOL SUBJECTS AND SUCCESS

Two other themes also feature in some girls' texts:
- the gendered constructs of school subjects that are still apparent in schools; and
- the gendered constructs of success and achievement.

These themes emerge specifically in the following girl's response:

> • Boys are expected to either be dumb or good at sport. If they're neither then they're kind of outcasts. It's easier to be smart at school if you're a girl but if girls want to do a mechanics class or metalwork they're in the minority. It's the same with boys and sewing or home economics too. But the boys just pretend they do cooking class so they can eat, and then it's ok (GHS F 1/15).

As girls in the government middle class co-educational school noted:

> • I wish boys and girls were treated the same e.g. not thought to be weaker and therefore have to do different sport, etc (GHSV F 53/16).

> • ... when moving furniture, we only need to carry chairs whilst guys seize the tables!! (GHSV F 114/16).

Some girls were aware of internal hierarchies of approval and affirmation based on subject choice and, even within a single sex school setting, it was apparent that some curricular areas were more rewarded than others:

> • They don't take art seriously enough. I don't mean music or drama. People who are good at that are always acknowledged. I mean visual art like painting ... I work so hard at being involved in art but I know I will never have a symbol on my blazer for that, unlike sporty girls for instance. They are rewarded for being passionate but not girls like me. I also think that boys' schools are a lot more advantaged than girls' schools. They offer amazing resources and endless amounts of subjects (SSGS 170/16).

Some girls from the affluent single sex school expressed a concern and anxiety about having to succeed in ways that reveal a particular classist construction of achievement (see Harris, 2004):

> • There's a lot of pressure at such a good school to get excellent grades and even though nobody says anything you can tell people really stress out (SSGS 33/15).

> • This school is way too strict and they have this problem with having to have the best reputation ... I would love to go to a high school where there is more freedom and more individuality (SSGS 64/15).

For those girls who did not invest in academic achievement or who had no aspirations to attend university, they felt pressured and found it difficult to be motivated at school:

> • The school assumes that we are all going to university and gives us the message that in order to achieve anything in life you must go to uni ... I have trouble finding the relevance in many classes to the real world. I want to spend my time doing something worthwhile,

earning money, working. But with pressure from school and parents, dropping out is not an option (SSGS 163/16).

TEACHERS TURNING 'A BLIND EYE' OR COLLUDING

Another issue that arose at this single sex school was the marginalisation felt by some girls whose family circumstances did not conform to the 'picture perfect' white middle class construction of families (see Carrington & Luke, 2002). This feeling of being misunderstood and marginal was exacerbated by teachers who did not take into account the effect of certain family structures and systems on girls' learning:

- I am from Italian and Greek backgrounds with divorced parents ... my life at home is often stressful, having to swap homes between parents is difficult. It is annoying and difficult when we have to be taken from one side of the family to the other side all the time for big wog events. These also distract me from my homework. It is difficult going to school with all these girls from picture perfect families who never have to worry about which clothes to pack for the week ahead and whether they've remembered their schoolbooks. Teachers aren't very understanding either. I always get picked on for forgetting books and uniforms - I'd like to see them try and stay organised when they have to set up and pack away so often (SSGS 170/16).

Some girls from various schools felt that teachers 'turn a blind eye' to the effects of the gendered and sex-based dimensions of harassment, which appear to be related to the hierarchical structuring of peer group relations at school:

- Being a girl is also hard. We have to deal with friends, bitchiness and boys giving us crap. I think that teachers turn a blind eye to this because all they care about is whether they teach their classes, the curriculum, so they do well in tests making themselves look good (CCHS F 95/14).

Thus, teachers are seen as being so professionally and personally invested in 'making themselves look good' through students' academic achievements that it is often at the expense of student health and well-being. Indeed, the following student indicates that teachers collude with those 'popular' students who are the instigators of such forms of harassment in that they dismiss their behaviour as 'just a joke' (see Alloway, 2000):

- School's alright, the only thing that really shits me is the 'popular' people believing that they can treat others like shit. I'm not really affected by this as I tell the 'popular' people where to go but there are others that are really picked on, just because they are 'unpopular' and everyone laughs and it's really cruel. I often stick up for these people but they have to do it themselves. The thing that makes it worse is the teachers do nothing, to them the 'popular' people are funny and harmless and that, when they pick on others, it's just a joke, but it's not. So therefore school is like a society of classes and clichés that think themselves above others (CCHS F 140/14).

Hence, teachers are perceived by some students as aligning themselves with the popular students against those who are being harassed. For example, the following girl sees teasing as a 'normal' part of school life – an expected and perhaps inevitable social practice in her eyes:

- I don't really experience many problems, maybe just the normal things like being teased (GHS F 87/15).

Interestingly, the only school where girls spoke positively of school counselling services and attention to student health and well-being was the single sex girls' school:

- Teachers are amazingly understanding and when people do have problems we never hesitate to go to our school counsellor (SSGS 102/16).

- We have more of an opportunity to see counsellors without being teased or bagged, unlike boys (SSGS 140/15).

Indeed, several girls specifically spoke about their school as a place of comfort and safety, so much so that leaving the school in the future appeared to be daunting:

- School for me is like a comfort zone (SSGS 113/16).

- School is like my little safety barrier. I come to school and I feel at home. I'm surrounded by friends and familiar faces … Honestly, the prospect of leaving school is quite daunting, even intimidating (SSGS 125/16).

- Girls are more open and can communicate well to teachers and peers without the fear of being embarrassed. This I find is a strength at this school being only girls (SSGS 53/15).

CONCLUSION

As we have illustrated in this chapter, girls' responses highlight that there are indeed pressing issues that need to be addressed for girls as well as boys at school and that school-based policies need to take these into consideration. For both boys and girls, what emerges is the significant impact of a school culture that positions students as subordinates in terms of its capacity to fuel passive and/or aggressive resistance and anti-school sentiments in the student body. As Quinlivan writes:

> Understandings of the multifarious and shifting ways in which students position themselves in relation to discourses of sexuality and gender and the interplay between the two discourses could provide valuable insights for teachers into how to meet the needs of young women in schools more effectively (1999: 66).

What also emerged as significant was the positive responses provided by many girls attending the single sex school in relation to a culture that was characterised by its commitment to creating a supportive learning and caring environment (Ancess, 2003). This was attributed to the school's acknowledgment of the links between girls' well-being and learning. From the girls' point of view, there was evidence of quality teaching, a culture of participation and achievement in a broad range of academic, cultural and social pursuits. Of particular significance in relation to the backlash construction of boys as 'the new disadvantaged' is the way some girls attributed the quality of their schooling to the absence of both boys and the institutionalisation of hegemonic masculinist systems of control, surveillance and regulation. However, girls in both single sex and co-educational schools did tend to highlight the very real effects of social hierarchies amongst girls and their impact on their lives at school.

GIRLS AND SCHOOL

AIM • To develop a deeper understanding about girls' experiences of school structures and culture

AUTHORITARIAN POWER

We need to acknowledge that some girls also actively resist authoritarian power structures at school. Girls also indicated that too much emphasis was placed on enforcing petty school rules as opposed to addressing their emotional health and welfare.

FOR REFLECTION

- To what extent do you think girls are stereotyped as passively conforming to school-based authority?

GENDER AND LEARNING

We need to understand that traditional notions of femininity impact on girls and how they negotiate their positions and are positioned within social hierarchies. Girls' social relationships with each other influence significantly the quality of their experience of life at school.

FOR REFLECTION

- How might issues of 'fitting in' for girls be addressed at a whole school level?

DISCUSSION FORUM

THEME 1 • THE IMPACT OF SCHOOL AND TEACHERS

Explore what the following girls say about teachers, pedagogy and learning. Are these issues evident in your school? How are they being addressed?

- Sometimes teachers don't ask or try to understand how a student feels. They expect a lot. Some teachers suck (CCHS F 101/14).

- School is not very good. It needs to be more interesting, fun and have us still learn things. If people are bored of what they are learning about they are going to disrupt everyone else to show that they are bored. I feel that if they made it fun they would participate more (GHS F 93/15).

- Personally I feel as though school is overrated. I hate the rules especially, I mean how does the number of earrings in your ears or whether or not you wear nail polish really affect your schoolwork/performance? What's the point of those pathetic rules anyway? Teachers are know-it-alls, they can't take criticism and if you correct them, it's considered cheeky! You can't even crack a joke in class without them accusing you of making fun of their teaching methods! (CCHS F 111/15).

- Sometimes the teachers don't pay attention to you, like they know who you are but it feels like you're invisible. It's so strict, I do not like it. I am not allowed to wear my religious cross which I got when I was a baby, sometimes they would take it off me and don't return it till the end of term! Not enough freedom, that's why students like me rebel. I feel like they treat us like babies. I know in life you have to have rules but some rules schools have are stupid! (SSGS 139/16).

- School is a load of crap! Teachers don't understand your problems and have no respect for your feelings. It's really hard when you have problems at home 'cause when you get to school teachers give you no time to talk to counsellors etc ... If teachers would stop fucking worrying about dumb uniforms and whether your top button is done up properly and start worrying about our health, etc ... School would be heaps easier, some TEACHERS ARE SEXIST PIGS. Mr X pervs on girls (CCHS F 129 /15).

- I get frustrated when teachers seem to care so much about correct uniform, completed homework, etc, when hundreds of people are dying every minute in wartorn third world countries. I have trouble completing irrelevant, boring homework and study when I remember this. My teachers just think I'm being rebellious and wicked but I can't handle the pointlessness (CCHS F 110/16).

THEME 2 • GIRLS' HEALTH AND WELL-BEING

What kinds of physical, social and emotional health issues impact on the following girls' lives at school? How could school-based policies and curriculum in relation to health and personal development address these issues?

- The school doesn't care about the well-being of the students, just their results (GHSV F 148/16).

- I drive a BMW and I live in the rich part of the city, but my life sometimes is so scary that I find it hard to breathe (SSGS 143/16).

- I don't mind school that much but sometimes I feel as though I'd rather die than go to school. For me, it's not the work or the teachers that make it hard, it's fellow students. If you don't live up to their expectations or give in to them, they can turn a whole group against you. There are also different social classes, which makes me feel worthless as I don't come from a wealthy family. I am always trying to be someone I'm not and I'm always self-conscious and shy in school, whereas out of school, I am confident and happy. I don't really experience many problems but the teachers all think we hate school because of the work. I can't speak for anyone else, but I think it's totally the opposite. They don't realise that we wag and are unhappy because of the social standings and growing up in school. My best friend for 11 years is the only person I feel close to and she is going through some problems right now but she has me and I have her. Sometimes that's all you can ask for outside of the classroom (GHS F 116/15).

- School for me is pretty annoying as in classes the teachers pick on me a lot and socially I feel that my friends abuse the friendship type thing. Being a girl at school is a pain because you are expected to do sport and be good at it and you have your popular groups and if you are not in these groups you are classed as being 'up yourself' or being a 'square' … In September last year I attempted suicide but didn't succeed. This year I have had problems everywhere. A lot of my friendships have fallen apart and I have become very isolated from everyone. My grades have gone down as I got put in certain classes that are too high for my ability and I blame a) my low self-esteem and b) my feeling of isolation at school. I literally hate school. I want to change schools but everyone says that the same thing will happen wherever I go (GHS F 85/15).

- At school being a girl can get real annoying. Every month for about a week we are in and out of the toilets or have to stay home and miss a lot of work. It makes it real hard to catch up. Girls get teased if people find out about it [menstruating] (GHS F 107/15).

THEME 3 • THE MEANINGS OF SUCCESS AND ACHIEVEMENT

What pressures do some girls experience in trying to be 'successful' and to 'achieve'? How does your school provide a variety of ways for students to experience 'achievement' and 'success'?

- There's a lot of pressure to be successful and have a good career (SSGS 51/15).

- The school gives us pressure to do well. Some teachers are only interested in good marks (SSGS 65/15).

- I do not enjoy school. I feel that once I leave school I believe I will be doing a manual hands on job e.g. hairdresser. Therefore things like Shakespeare don't affect me ... I just don't suit this fake snobby atmosphere. I get scared about exams and I don't want to fail but struggle to get motivated to work (SSGS 158/17).

THEME 4 • INTERPLAY OF MULTIPLE INFLUENCES ON GIRLS' LIVES AT SCHOOL

Using this case study, discuss how multiple factors intersect and impact on girls' relationships with others, their learning and their emotional health. Are these factors evident or are you aware of these issues in the lives of girls at your school? How might these issues be addressed in schools?

- Being a girl at school is kind of hard in places, but it just depends how you deal with it. There are always the 'popular chicks' (that does not include me) to deal with and I sometimes get quite a lot of crap from them. For me, I deal with it pretty easy by just ignoring them, but I've known other girls who have been really depressed because they are not popular or they were made fun of. The guys are pretty much the same, some can give you a really hard time but others are really supportive. My main problem at school now is that being smart seems to appeal to some people as a sign that says 'pick on me'. I'm not sure what it is but if you're smart you'll get picked on. Tall poppy syndrome I guess. As an Asian student, there really isn't any problem for me ... School for me is sometimes like sinking or getting stuck in quicksand. Sometimes you feel so weighed down and the more you fight it, the more you sink ... Conflicts at school are the worst. You could say they are caused by differences in maturity and values between genders and different people. Some issues (especially sex-related ones) come up often and somehow people think it hurts me when they ridicule my sexuality. I'm straight but I have no problem with people who choose otherwise. Some girls can be real bitches. The problem is, everyone else (including teachers) think they are 'cool' so you kind of get stuck. Climbing the social hierarchy in school isn't a priority for me but for others it is a big deal. Relationships are becoming a big deal now – with friends and the opposite sex. Unfortunately the emphasis by the 'popular chicks' is on sex and because these girls become the 'main talk' guys tend to think that you are like them. In summary, school is more than just about education at the academic level, there is a complex social hierarchy present and severe cases of tall poppy syndrome. Issues such as puberty, sexuality and relationships must be dealt with and it isn't always easy (CCHS F 93/15/Chinese-Malaysian).

3

BEING A BOY
'Guys can be like dogs and sniff you out fast'

- One of the other major issues is to be cool and macho in a world where those who play sport and are strong are supreme and those skinny, 'four-eyed nerds' are the 'underworld rats' (SSBS 4/16).

IN THIS CHAPTER YOU WILL:

- learn more about the policing of masculinity in boys' lives at school;
- develop a deeper understanding about the role that homophobia and 'being cool' plays in boys' lives at school;
- engage in a Professional Development session using boys' voices to build knowledge about the impact of gender and sexuality on their developing understanding about what it means to be a boy.

INTRODUCTION

The regulation and policing of gender for both boys and girls emerged as a major issue impacting on the experiences of schooling for many students across all the schools we surveyed. Our research follows on from the work of Lees (1993), Mac an Ghaill (1994), Epstein (1997), Gilbert & Gilbert (1998), Haag (1999) and Francis (2000) who have documented the various ways in which gender normalisation has impacted on boys and girls' lives at school. Davies, for example, speaks about this in terms of 'category maintenance work' (1989: 29), which refers to the policing of the boundaries of acceptable and desirable versions of masculinity and femininity (see also Martino, 2000).

Within these frames of reference (as indicated in the introduction), we deploy students' voices in a deliberate and strategic attempt to disrupt the rhetoric informing many of the populist debates about the boys – a rhetoric often propagated by adult men talking about or on behalf of boys. This involves viewing boys through a normative and normalising lens, without differentiating between hierarchical versions of masculinity. It also means fogging the lens and averting the normalising gaze away from how normative masculinist school structures and cultures construct, perpetuate and ignore the homophobia and misogyny that lead to bullying and resistance to learning for many boys (Mills, 2001; Martino & Pallotta-Chiarolli, 2003). Within backlash discourses driving the boys' education agenda, the emphasis is on the need to defeminise schooling in order to improve educational outcomes for boys. What is denied or erased is how bullying and resistance to learning for boys is symptomatic of the hegemonic masculinist structures and cultures still legitimated in schools and manifested through homophobia and misogyny (see Salisbury & Jackson, 1996; Epstein 1997; Jackson, 1998; Lingard & Douglas, 1999).

THE IMPACT OF BEING A 'NORMAL' BOY AT SCHOOL

One of the major issues for boys who took part in our research, apart from their criticism of teachers and the kinds of power relations enforced at school, related to the impact of normalisation and normative masculinity on their lives. Boys constructed themselves and were constructed by others as either adhering to a powerful performance of dominant normative masculinity or displaying traits and signs of transgressive masculinity, usually in relation to being seen as 'girlie or gay'. This hierarchical binary emerged for many boys in their reference to the prevalence of homophobia and bullying at school, as well as its impact on learning (see Dorais, 2004). As the research has shown, the requirement to display one's self as appropriately heterosexual often informs the ways in which many boys learn to police their masculinities (see Mac an Ghaill, 1994; Epstein, 1997; Plummer, 1999; Gilbert & Gilbert, 1998; Martino, 2000; Martino & Pallotta-Chiarolli, 2003). The role that homophobia plays in this practice of defining and negotiating masculinities was highlighted by many of the boys in our research. Homophobia was often mentioned as a pervasive and inevitable part of the boys' lives at school, and a major strategy of boundary demarcation between the normative and transgressive boys. This was indicated by a number of boys from the single sex boys' school:

- It's shit being a boy at an all-boys school, you have to conform to the stereotype or you're 'GAY' and the people that aren't in the 'COOL' group are treated like shit (SSBS 1/16).

- This school is very bad. Our parents waste over $8000 dollars a year and the learning environment is substandard to other schools in this area. It is a proven fact that boys at this all-boys school have the worst education of all co-ed, all-girls or all-boys schools. It is impossible to do any work at this school without being singled out as a nerd ... Not having a co-ed school makes a homophobic society. The whole X school culture is stuffed up. X school boys call anyone who they don't like 'gay'. The word is used so much it no longer has meaning (SSBS 15/16).

Some boys were wary of the possibility that there might be gay or same-sex attracted boys at their school, or were aware of the harassment that a gay student would receive if they came out:

- Well to answer your question school is fucked. Being a guy means you have to watch out for homosexuals (SSBS 44/16).

- We are all boys and the only problems we have to deal with is wondering if there are any gay people in the school (SSBS 33/17).

- Boys don't have to deal with anything but I think that if you were gay you would have a really hard time (GHSV M 34/16).

These responses highlight the homophobic surveillance of boys at school and, hence, the category boundary maintenance work that is carried out by the dominant group that performs and perpetuates a conformist compulsory heterosexual masculinity (Frank, 1987; 1993). This results in the policing of any form of transgressive masculinity that may be an indicator of homosexuality. In the following, a boy from the Catholic co-educational school writes about boys 'sniffing out' their peers who deviate from normative masculinity. As a boy who is constructed and related to as a transgressive male, he discusses the effects of such border patrolling (see Steinberg et al., 1997):

- I get the occasional snigger, tease 'Faggot, gay etc' because I'm real expressive and very in touch with my feminine side. I'm not gay, but I have three sisters, and I can relate and understand them very well. I'm very sensitive too, and at school guys can be like dogs and sniff you out fast. If you stuff up in the sense of wearing the wrong shoes, clothes, friends, you can cop a whole heap of shit. But the action of those guys are out of fear of not conforming to the pathetic egoistic standards. Being a guy that isn't popular, if you don't fit in, then you're immediately labelled. What you usually find [is] that the way to harass a guy's dignity is to affect his sexuality. Common issues of insults could be 'faggot, gay, homo, sped, etc' really insulting names. For guys it's also an ego thing. Who's the most

> heroic, bravest, who can pick up the best chick, who can cop a root or a bit ... first. The peer pressure is pretty strong. You will find that all of the guys are very afraid. You can get the strongest looking guy, but he's still afraid. Guys think that they have to fit in. I do, sometimes, but I guess I'm realising that it's not worth it, and plus I think, why would I want to be like them. I wish that guys could be more individual, because only then, I think the issues mentioned wouldn't occur often (CCHS M 2/15).

Another boy from the rural school also discusses the homophobic harassment that he is subjected to, which appears to be related to his (transgressive) involvement in singing and drama at school:

> - School for me means a place where I learn but also get harassed about my sexuality, even though I'm not, I still get called gay and poofta and other degrading names, but now I am strong enough to ignore the minorities and look to my future and other talents, like my singing which I only found out I could do when I came to high school, I've been singing for 4 years now and have sung in front of the school and entered eisteddfods and got places so I think that is more important than worrying about stupid kids ... that schools today are forced to accommodate (RSHS M 6/15).

Transgressing the boundaries of what is considered to be acceptable masculinity leads to harassment of those boys who fail to measure up. One gay identifying student commented that even teachers at his school 'singled him out':

> - Yes, I do experience problems at school. Being picked on, beaten up, sledged, and being singled out from my peers. I'm gay and people think it is wrong or bad to be gay but I don't think it is. My boyfriend cops the same treatment at his school. Even some of the teachers at school single me out and that really gets on

my nerves. I sit by myself all day in the playground at recess and lunch and in the classroom (RGHS M 3/16).

One of the most significant responses which captured the nature of the power dynamics of compulsory heterosexuality governing the ways in which boys learn to relate socially at school was provided by this student:

- Being a boy is just normal apart from not wanting to act or look like a faggot. You don't want to get crap from anyone ... Issues are not wanting to be the target of a group who continually gives you crap, there aren't any other issues I know of unless you do something like cry or act gay, that can give you a reputation you can't live down (CCHS M 1/15).

'MACHO BULLSHIT'

Many boys wrote about the regimes of bullying and harassment that were so much a part of being a boy at school. These practices were often explicitly linked to the 'macho bullshit' that many boys felt they were expected to subscribe to in order to be constructed and related to as 'normal' boys:

- Guys have to put up with macho bullshit. It's pathetic how these idiots can run the shit the way they do (SSBS 9/17).

- At a boys' school, athletic ability and strength plays a large role in how many mates and how popular you are. So if you're fat and a spastic you're doomed to eternal rejection (SSBS 2/16).

- Being a boy means that if you don't act macho you get given crap. Boys don't really have any ways to deal with problems because there is no outlet for emotions and no-one to talk to about issues. I get depressed a lot and the only way to stop it is to get really angry which means I tend to offend other people a lot and be really mean to them. I can't really talk about problems and feel trapped a lot (CCHS M 3/14).

- In an all-boys school there is always the issue of bullying, I have to admit, I too have bullied, hey it's mean, but the reason for this is so that we can toughen up those who are weak. I'm quiet however no-one picks on me as I'm a complete beefcake! - not fat just well-built (SSBS 3/16).

CCHS 3's response is significant in that it links to the issue of not being able to deal with his emotions and of feeling trapped because of this. He seems to be highlighting the need for emotional support, the lack of which is connected for him to depression and associated practices of masculinity involving harassment and bullying. SSBS 2 also highlights the role of sport as a social practice through which many boys learn to validate their masculinity and to gain the status of being 'tough' or 'cool' through enforcing a distinction from those subordinated boys considered to be inferior. SSBS 3 specifically talks about the role of the body in enacting such versions of masculinity in his reference to being a 'complete beefcake'. He makes the point that despite the fact he is quiet, he is able to avoid the attribution of associative weakness due to being well-built. These regimes of hierarchical binarily constructed power relations amongst boys are also given a certain emphasis by a student with a disability at the rural school:

- School is a place where you become popular or you don't because of peer pressure. Peer pressure has been a major role in my life since I first started school, people have always given me a hard time because I chose not to do some of the things or activities that they chose to do ... For example, I am not a good sports player yet I like to play it, but I have a problem with me which means that I am unable to do stuff like that properly. And so I cop all of my peers' abuse because I am not good at sport and this really pisses me off

because I don't want to tell them that I am slow and
also poorly co-ordinated because then they will in turn
treat me different again, but that's the way the cycle
works and now as I get old my problems get worse
because my back is starting to go on me and I will be in
a wheelchair by the time I am 25 ... So as my peers
push me down as I try my best to do things, I run out
of choices. I have tried to kill myself twice and I am
getting to that stage again where I feel that everything I do is wrong, I can't get anything right ... hopefully I should live to keep you up to date with my life
and its happenings (RGHS M 2/16/Disabled).

Another student also highlights how boys undertake a kind of surveillance of their peers' masculinity which involves a focus on the body, with particular attention being devoted to physical strength, penis size and body weight:

• An issue that boys have to deal with a lot is how
strong they are. Often boys will just start pushing each
other for no reason and if you show that you are hurt
by what they have done then they will keep on doing it
to you until you do something back to them. Also if a
boy looks weak but is actually strong but people don't
know he is strong then they will call him lanky, weak,
faggot and other abusive names. Also if people hide in
the change rooms to get changed and people begin to
notice it then that person is called Pin Dick or is given
crap if they are fat, then people start talking about
them having big tits and a fat ass (CCHS M 54/15).

The following boy mentions that teachers do not appear to be aware of the effects of such practices of all-embracing conformist masculinity and of how they impact on the lives of students at school, particularly those boys who are positioned as transgressive and 'other':

• Boys have to stand up for themselves and their
friends to the people who feel they are cool ... Boys

have to make themselves look either big or insignificant to avoid bullying and pressure. However, if people stick together then they are less likely to be the ones pressured. As this is an easy solution, groups begin to form in the school, which either help each other out or go in search of someone else to attack. Half of the teachers have no idea of what's going on and nothing is done about it (CCHS M 45/14).

ACTING 'COOL'

Time and time again boys spoke of the pressure that was placed on them to act and behave in a certain way according to the dictates of hegemonic heterosexual masculinity (Frank, 1987; Jackson, 1998):

- Being a boy in school is hard, you have constant abuse from the so-called 'popular kids' and pressures to conform. If we don't conform or perform we will be nagged and made fun of more. Boys have to face issues like to like the 'right girls', to be socially acceptable, to be sporty and not brainy (CCHS M 38/15).

- At school boys have to wear a mask, girls crying and showing emotion would be comforted by friends. Although if a boy were to do this he would be rejected by his friends and peers. This is one issue that just boys have to deal with at school (CCHS M 10/15).

- What issues do boys have to face ... not looking like a fairy ... not being too dumb ... not being too smart ... every pressure available ... fitting in the right groups ... No matter how hard you try and how much effort you put in you always end up back at the bottom ... girls are more in touch with their feelings and have learnt to express it ... they [boys] can be left emotionally scarred ... to fit in is the hardest thing of all (CCHS M 24/16).

- Being a boy, you have to learn to stick up for yourself, learn a few comeback lines in case someone is teasing you. The main issue you have to deal with is verbal abuse, everyone is teased at school at least once and yes, verbal abuse can lead to full or physical fights. You have to learn not to push people to the edge, and learn to come up with comeback lines. Another issue you have to deal with is drugs (GHS M 233/14).

The following boy, like many others, highlights how 'acting cool' is also about practices of performing masculinity which involve being 'a troublemaker' and/or undertaking risk-taking behaviours such as doing drugs to 'show off' to your mates. Although these behaviours could be constructed and defined as socially transgressive, this transgression is redefined as evidence and status-marking of a normative masculinity (see Martino & Pallotta-Chiarolli, 2003). Some boys also mention the increasing pressure placed on boys to have sex with girls:

- Boys are very competitive especially in the sporting field, those who are not very talented are subjected to embarrassment of not making the team. Drugs seem to be an increasing problem because everyone 'thinks' it's cool to do it, frankly I feel drugs are pretty sad and done only to 'show off' to mates. Girls are an interesting factor at school, being a 'handsome' young man I pull chicks pretty easy. Some find it hard though, and are subjected to being called 'fags' simply because they are not as confident as others. Also there has become increasing pressure to do more with a girl. For instance 'kissing' is simply not enough, one is now expected at least to 'go down' or receive oral. Some are pressured into this when really they are not old enough or experienced in such sexual acts (SSBS 4/16).

What is emphasised is once again the effects of certain normalising tendencies that are built into how boys are expected to behave at school and the role of the peer group in these social practices of masculinity (see Kehily & Nayak, 1997; Martino & Meyenn, 2001).

There is an emphasis on proving one's self through competitive sport and pressure to 'do drugs', which appear to be requirements for successfully displaying proper masculinity. However, 'acting cool' is inevitably linked to regimes of compulsory heterosexuality (Rich, 1980) where failure to 'pull chicks' runs the risk of being subjected to homophobic harassment, thus highlighting the importance many boys felt in our study of 'not wanting to act or look like a faggot'.

These forms of gender-based harassment had a major impact on many boys' lives at school:

- I came from Indonesia, and I was amazed (not surprised amazed, crappy amazed) how different life is. Where I come from, nobody gives people shit, tease or bully them. When I came here people give me shit, even some of my friends punch me. I'm not accustomed to punching. I'm just so different. Being at school is like going to the army because boys have been brought up to a custom, there are groups around the school – surfers, the wogs, the nerds and the rejects. I'm not saying that I am in the rejects, no, it's because I feel like a reject. Being given shit all this time is not jolly. You feel left out ... you can't be fat and then friends will give you shit for being fat. You can't be a try hard or else shit. Everything has to be nice and doody. If you do something bad everybody gives you shit forever, they remember it ... if you wear surfie shirt, cargo pants ... if you wear something different, they 'brand' you techno, rapper. What is this?!! This is bullshit!! Why do people brand you? Some of my friends want me to be something I'm not, that's why I feel bad all the time. I don't have good skill at sport, I play tennis well and I'm not very smart but what does that mean to people, JACK SHIT!! because if you're not smart or attractive or good at sport you're basically a reject, a piece of shit. This is basically a typical old stereotyping, I can't believe it still exists today ... I experience a lot of problems, firstly my friends don't treat me as they should ... they treat me like shit (CCHS M 14/16/Indonesian-Chinese).

This boy highlights the extent to which bullying and harassment is about normalisation – those who are considered not to fit the norm are harassed. One must also wear the right clothes and play the right sport. CCHS 14 seems to be highlighting that 'giving other people shit' also plays a significant role in how boys fashion their masculinities in peer group situations. It is a means by which they can get a laugh at the expense of someone else who becomes the butt of the put-downs (see Kehily and Nayak, 1997). What also needs to be interrogated here is the extent to which these normative constructions of a hegemonic masculinity are being read as hierarchical Anglo-Australian versions of masculinity that lead to the inferiorisation and marginalisation of some boys from culturally diverse backgrounds (see Martino & Pallotta-Chiarolli, 2003).

Many girls corroborated these findings about boys' social relationships:

- Boys try harder to be liked – they find more confidence in themselves by making a fool of either themselves or another person just to be liked – to get a laugh out of their peers. The only reason popular kids have such an effect on unpopular kids is because the unpopular kids let them – none of them have the confidence to speak up (CCHS F 180/15).

- If I was a boy I'd be conscious of my body, I know there is so much pressure for boys to have muscles, etc and for boys who don't have that kind of build it would be really hard for them (SSGS 130/16).

- Boys usually try to hard to impress the girls and make us want to laugh. I just reckon they should act normal (GHSV F 194/16).

The comment made by GHSV 194 is of particular interest in that it highlights her construction of boys as staging a particular masculine performance which she does not classify as 'normal', as somehow not 'natural'. Is this girl indicating her awareness that there is something forced and highly scripted about the way many boys publicly perform their masculinity, especially for the purpose of 'impressing' girls?

CONCLUSION

This chapter has pointed to the very significant influence of homophobia in terms of its capacity to regulate boys' behaviour and their understanding of 'acceptable' or 'normal' masculinity. It highlights how boys may police and demarcate transgressive masculinity in order not to be targeted for harassment (Martino, 2000). The issue appears to be one related to surveillance of those boys who do not embody or perform acceptable heterosexual masculinities. This has important implications for addressing bullying in schools, particularly with regards to developing school-based policies which name the sex- and gender-based dimensions of harassment (see Collins et al., 1996; Laskey & Beavis, 1996; Beckett, 1998; Alloway, 2000; Davison, 2000; Mills, 2001). It also raises questions about school structures, cultures and curricula that promote and perpetuate a sex/gender system which then gets played out among boys. Yet adult and educational cultures and systems are not examined critically within backlash educational politics and debates. For instance, in *Boys' education: Getting it right,* homophobia and its impact on boys' peer relations, well-being and learning was not mentioned (House of Representatives Standing Committee, 2002). However, our research and the research of so many others highlights the pervasive role that homophobia plays in boys' lives at school (Frank, 1993; Mac an Ghaill, 1994; Epstein, 1997; Plummer, 1999; Davison, 2000; Mills, 2001; Martino & Pallotta-Chiarolli, 2003; Renold, 2003; Dorais, 2004; McNinch & Cronin, 2004; Pallotta-Chiarolli, 2005b).

BEING A BOY

AIM • To develop a deep understanding about the impact of masculinity on boys' lives at school

NORMALISATION

Normalisation impacts significantly on boys' experiences of 'being a boy' or masculinity at school.

What it means to be a 'normal' boy often entails rejecting any association with the feminine or with being gay.

Acting cool often involves subscribing to dominant masculinity. This can involve acting tough, impressing mates, using put-downs, homophobia and sexism as a form of humour.

GENDER-BASED HARASSMENT AND CONSTRAINT

Dominant notions of masculinity can lead to boys feeling compelled to assert their heterosexuality. This can result in gender-based harassment and marginalisation of those boys who do not measure up to what is considered to be appropriate or desirable masculinity.

Dominant masculinity, while conferring power and status, often leads to some boys feeling constrained and trapped.

REJECTING 'MACHO BULLSHIT'

Not all boys subscribe to dominant masculinity and in fact reject being 'cool'. They realise that masculine behaviour can be oppressive and limiting.

DISCUSSION FORUM

Based on the responses below, how would you define masculinity or what it means to be a boy? What versions of masculinity are considered to be 'normal' and desirable in the dominant adult culture? How might school-based policies address these kinds of questions?

What social expectations related to being a boy impact upon these students' lives? How do some of these boys try to resist dominant versions of masculinity? How do school policies, curricula and culture support those boys who resist this kind of masculinity, or who are marginalised because of it?

To what extent does your school reinforce a very narrow version of masculinity? What role do official school structures (such as assemblies, newsletters, extracurricula activities), as well as the 'hidden curriculum', play in encouraging boys to embrace a broader definition of masculinity, or what it means to be a boy?

Are the following terms named and addressed in student welfare/pastoral care policies and curricula at your school: the pecking order and social hierarchies of masculinities, dominant and marginalised versions of masculinities, homophobia, femiphobia, heterosexism, compulsory heterosexuality?

> • Being a boy at this school has its stereotypes you have to fulfil. You're looked down upon if you're mentally disabled, or not 'macho' or [don't] take an active interest in girls (if not, you're considered gay) ... I'm a pacifist. I hate violence and I try my best never to put down anybody. I always try to say something encouraging, I guess that's my nature. I think also that boys have to deal with the issues of 'fitting in' into groups ... Boys have to try to be rough and tough and swear. I always get so much crap because I don't do that kinda stuff. I've also been described as 'very naive and ignorant in the sex department'. Boys have to be wanting to

be interested in pornographic girls. I find that stuff very filthy and I thank my parents so much for protecting me from this kinda stuff. People have been contemplating whether I was gay.

I personally hate humanity and how they act. School life is full of spiteful people and if I could get a private tutor to get me through high school, I would. I dislike people at this school (CCHS M 11/14).

- At school if you are a boy and you want to be popular you have to get in trouble with teachers and take drugs and stuff like that to be in the cool group and you also have to be tough. The issues that boys have to deal with is peer pressure and that is about it. The girls have to look good to be in the popular group and the boys have to be bad in school to be in the popular group (CCHS M 30/15).

- I suppose the issues that boys deal with mainly is bullying and pressure to be 'trouble makers' (CCHS M 36/15).

- I have come from a different country to learn in another one that I hardly know anything about, I think that boys are faced with the dilemma that they have to live up to their friends' expectations and not their own, i.e. they have to be macho and have to be brutal all the time when in actual fact they aren't, but if they don't act like that they are considered a faggot or gay!!! (GHS M 269/16/South African).

- Being a boy at school is harder than being a girl. Some issues boys have to deal with are being good at sport, not hitting girls, coping with sexist teachers and putting up with people questioning your sexuality. Boys just deal with issues relating to teachers and sport, whilst girls just have to worry about their friends. The issues boys have to deal with are harder because people expect boys to be good at sport, to be tough, not to hit girls, to be dumb and to misbehave. If you don't fit this stereotype then you get picked on. For girls issues like these just aren't there and they have it much easier (GHS M 221/15).

● Boys deal with the pressure to pick up girls and get far with them on weekends (GHSV M 197/16).

● Boys seem to have more of a friendship problem than girls – i.e. they always have to prove to each other how good they are, and pressure everyone to do the same thing – they don't have any minds of their own (CCHS F 182/16).

4

BEING A GIRL
'It really all depends on what type of girl you are!'

- Being a girl at school can be hard sometimes. You have your 'first class' society, your 'second class', 'average class' and your old-fashioned 'nerds' very stereotypical, yes, but true. Your 'first class' girls are considered as 'gorgeous' and 'good figured', or who are the most talked about by guys. If you're into the drugs/drinking scene, you're one of them. If you've been out with the most popular guys, you're one of them (CCHS F 96/15).

IN THIS CHAPTER YOU WILL:

- learn more about the policing of femininity in girls' lives at school;
- develop a deeper understanding about the role that sexuality and 'being cool' plays in girls' lives at school;
- engage in a Professional Development session using girls' voices to build knowledge about the impact of gender and sexuality on their developing understanding about what it means to be a girl.

INTRODUCTION

In the previous chapter, we have seen how homophobia featured significantly for boys in writing about their lives at school, and the boundary-demarcation between embracing and transgressing normative masculinity. In this chapter, and the following chapters, we will explore how the major issues for girls are related to the focus on the body and (hetero)sexual expression. The constant assertion of traditional norms governing the self-policing practices of the body with regards to appearance, body weight and body image were implicated in most girls' lives:

- Girls are expected to look pretty, be thin and have a large chest (GHS F 51/14).

- Girls are very sensitive about what others think of their weight. Some go anorexic over the issues of being told they're fat by peers (CCHS F 90/14).

We highlight how these norms are used to police desirable femininities and to delineate between traditional or normative femininity and transgressive femininity. What becomes apparent is that traditional or normative femininity, based on constructs of compliance, being a 'good girl', and sexual passivity, are derided by many girls as 'uncool' and 'loserish'. However, transgressive femininity, based on traditionally normative masculinist constructs such as sexual aggression, risk-taking behaviours and resistance to authority, are increasingly being viewed by girls as desirable and 'cool'. This is a direct inversion of the normative/transgressive masculinity binary for boys whereby conforming to a normative masculinity is 'cool' and transgressing normative masculinity is 'gay'.

The following piece of writing opened itself to multiple readings by us as researchers in relation to whether we were reading an example of normative masculinity or 'transgressive femininity'.

- I like smoking in the toilets and I like having sex in the toilets and enjoy giving oral sex ... I hate it when they [guys] grab my arse but I like it when they grab my boobs (GHSV F 68/16).

On the cover of the survey the student had initially ticked 'boy' as the gender identity. This was then scribbled out and corrected to indicate the opposite gender. Given that this survey was filled in as part of a school group wherein several boys constructed texts that seemed intended to shock the researchers, a possible reading is that it could be a boy masquerading as a girl, thereby performing a traditional normative hegemonic masculinity for his peers and for us, the researchers. Of course, if it is a girl, the main intent may also have been to shock the researchers. Is this an example of 'transgressive femininity' where the girl lists a range of behaviours she enjoys? Is she deliberately transgressing traditional notions of the 'good girl' who does not discuss or declare, let alone engage, in sex. She also breaks basic school rules about what can occur on school sites: she smokes in the toilets, claims to have sex in toilets. However, what is also in need of attention is how, if it is a girl, her sexual assertiveness is still very much defined and framed by boys' desires and behaviours: she talks about 'giving' rather than receiving oral sex, and indicates a particular way that boys approach her body, they 'grab' her body parts, in ways that she both 'hates' and 'likes'.

TRANSGRESSING OR ACCOMMODATING 'NORMAL' FEMININITY

It appears that whether girls are classified and self-define as 'nice girl' or 'bad girl', 'frigid' or 'slut', the issues of body image and appearance impacted upon all girls. Similarly, hierarchies and classifications related to body image and sexual expression for girls who subscribed to either traditional or transgressive femininities appear to be linked to normative masculinity. As one girl in our research said, 'boys have a major role in determining the social status of a girl'. Kenway et al. write about 'the sorts of femininities which unwittingly underwrite hegemonic masculinity' (1997: 120; see also Day et al., 2004). Reay also found that the girls in her study 'took up very varied positions in relation to traditional femininities. Yet, despite widely differentiated practices, all the girls at various times acted in ways which bolstered boys' power at the expense of their own' (2001: 153). She classified the girls in her primary school study into 'nice girls' who studied hard, were quiet and compliant, and were sexually restrained; the 'girlies' who fashioned their clothing, hair and make-up according to ultra-feminine media-inspired images; the 'spice girls' who transgressed the passivity of the 'nice, naïve girls' by being sexually aggressive and harassing boys; and the 'tomboys' who denigrated girls and preferred to be with boys doing and upholding 'boy things'. Some girls are endeavouring to emulate normative masculinist behaviours and attitudes associated with the power and dominance granted to boys. In this way, they feel that they are able to *gain* some social power in aligning themselves with normative masculinities through first, sexual relationships with boys; and second, harassing other boys and girls alongside the 'cool' boys in order to *share* in some of the social power pie.

In Reay's (2001) study, the 'girlies', with their 'emphasised femininity' (Connell, 1987: 187) were heavily involved in gender work which inscribed traditional heterosexual relations. Both the 'girlies' and the 'nice girls' were subject to 'discourses of denigration' by other girls and boys (Blackmore, 1999: 136). The 'nice girls' were unpopular for being hard-working and sexually chaste, 'boring' and 'nerdy', while the 'girlies' were described by boys as 'stupid' and 'dumb'. The 'spice girls' espousal of 'girl power' meant enthusiastically partaking in the boyfriend/girlfriend games, but they also operated 'beyond the boundaries of the girlies' more conformist behaviour when it came to the interaction with the boys' such as playing 'rating the boys', their 'favorite playground game'. One of the girls in Reay's study explained the game: 'you follow the boys around and give them a mark out of ten for how attractive they are' (2001: 160). Their philosophy was about 'giving as good as they got'. In relation to the 'tomboys', Reay believes that while:

> ... it is important to recognize the transgressive qualities of identifying and rejecting traditional notions of femininity ... the empowering aspects of being a 'tomboy' also masked deeply reactionary features ... Implicit in the concept of 'tomboy' is a devaluing of traditional notions of femininity, a railing against the perceived limitations of being female (2001: 163).

Implicit in some girls' responses in our research was a denigration of constructs of femininity and a valorising of traditional normative forms of masculinity:

- I find it really easy to make friends with guys. Girls have too many issues (GHSV F 202/16).

- I feel there would be less bitchiness if there were boys (SSGS 41/15).

- Girls are born bitches ... boys are much more straightforward (SSGS 146/16).

Thus, as Reay concludes, 'The means of accommodation may differ but the compliance with existing gender regimes remains ... boys maintain the hierarchy of social superiority of masculinity by devaluing the female world', either by the subordination of girls to the boys, or by girls devaluing girls and being acquiescent in prevailing gender hierarchies rather than being able to 'transform the gender divide'. Thus, 'the radical aspects of transgressive femininities ... are undermined by their implicit compliance with gender hierarchies'. Girls find themselves *ventriloquising* 'the dominant culture's denigration of femininity and female relations [which] can serve to disconnect them from other girls'. Resisting traditional discourses of subordinate femininity and attempting to take up powerful positions appears to come about 'through articulation with, and investment in, dominant masculinities [which] serves to reinforce rather than transform the gender divide' (2001: 163). Thus, 'a significant number of girls, if not subscribing to the view that boys are better, adhered to the view that it is better being a boy' (2001: 164). 'For much of the time, girls are 'trapped in the very contradictions they would transcend' and are 'drawn into making masculinity powerful' (Holland et al., 1998: 30).

As some girls have said in the workshops and seminars we give around Australia, it is now 'cool to be more like a guy but in a girlie way'. In other words, being sexually aggressive, harassing others considered inferior to one's 'cool' group, binge-drinking and smoking, sabotaging others' learning efforts and being overtly resistant or apathetic to learning are 'guys stuff' that girls are 'allowed' to co-opt within a feminine heterosexual performance. Such a performance is dependent upon and subordinate to normative masculinity (see Day et al., 2004). However, girls (and boys) indicate that there is a strong line that is policed between this form of acceptable transgressive femininity and forms of transgression that expose girls to labelling and harassment as 'dykes, sluts and butch'. Two other labels discussed in these workshops that are identified by girls as forms of 'acceptable' transgressive femininity are 'bitch Barbies' and 'Paris Hiltons'. Implicit in both these labels is an unquestioned and unquestionable form of embodied and fashioned dominant femininity, which is based on harassing and policing others in acceptable feminine ways through practices defined as 'bitching'. This occurs around issues of class, body image, clothing, and the display of nonchalance and put-down humour directed at the vulnerabilities, work efforts and lifestyles of others. Of course, the role of the media and popular culture is strongly evident here and draws attention to the adult cultures and powers that promote and commodify certain forms of femininity (see Harris, 2004).

These significant shifts and developments in the range of femininities made available to girls, according to what normative masculinity prescribes and permits, is being increasingly acknowledged in research (Harris et al., 2000; Reay, 2001; Tolman, 2002; Harris, 2004). Yet they are not apparent or adequately addressed in any backlash educational debates.

> At a time when we are told that there is a 'war on boys' and that girls are just fine, the voices of the girls in [Tolman's American] study sound a different note, reminding us that being a girl, living comfortably in a girl's body, is neither easy nor especially safe ... the socially manufactured dilemma of desire, which pits girls' embodied knowledge and feelings, their sexual pleasure and connection to their own bodies and to others through their desire, against physical, social, material, and psychological dangers associated with their sexuality ... (Tolman, 2002: 188).

Although some policies and debates in relation to the 'boys as victims' discourse will happily point to how feminism has given rise to 'overconfident' aggressive girls who bully boys, there is no acknowledgment of the normative masculinist power and expectations of femininity that frame and endorse the development and performance of a particular 'appropriately transgressive' femininity:

girls ... need to be protected from boys while also being attractive for boys ... girls are the objects of boys' sexual desires and have no desires of their own ... As a society, we parcel sexuality out, assuming that normal boys but not girls have 'raging hormones' ... We have effectively desexualized girls' sexuality (Tolman, 2002: 5).

SELF-REGULATION AND THE POLICING OF FEMININITY

Whether girls in our study perform a traditional or transgressive femininity, the body, appearance and sexuality emerged as major concerns in their lives, indicating the extent to which they had internalised an idealised image of embodied femininity. Here, we focus specifically on the anxiety-provoking discourses of the body and how this featured as a significant influence in the way many girls fashioned and negotiated their femininities through engaging in self-regulatory practices (Pallotta-Chiarolli, 1998). Harris et al. identify 'heteronomy, body management and responsibility' as among the persistent social regulations structuring young women's experiences within the sphere of heterosexuality (2000: 373). While they outline some of the ways in which girls accommodate these normative discourses, their research, like ours, also identifies ways in which girls resist, subvert and rework these discourses to create different ways of negotiating femininity and heterosexuality. The hegemonic definition of sexual maturity 'is often prescriptive, limiting and oppressive to young women' (Harris et al., 2000: 375). In particular, to be seen as 'properly female' requires young women:

> ... to tread very fine lines to emphasize their heterosexual desire, without actually doing too much heterosexual activity, in order to be perceived as mature ... women are dependent on men, derive sexual identity through managing their bodies with male desires in mind, but are simultaneously responsible for the sphere of sexual relations (2000: 375–76).

Girls are expected to 'act sensibly, patiently and rationally in sexual encounters, to keep their desires at bay, while boys are uncontrollable even to themselves' (2000: 377). Responsibility extends to controlling and managing unwanted as well as desired heterosexual contact (Pallotta-Chiarolli, 1998). For example, young women

> must monitor and control what can and cannot be seen, and be responsible for the effects of the sexual meaning of their body parts in social relations ... they learn to restrict their movement so as to preserve 'modesty' and to attempt to create a neutrality of their bodies to allow them to do everyday activities without the ascription of sexual meaning (Harris et al., 2000: 377).

Examples of being conscious and anxious about the 'sexual meaning of their body parts' were particularly evident in girls from co-educational schools:

- It annoys me when the girls wear their skirts/dresses so high that you can see their underwear (GHSV F 70/16).

- I hate windy days when your skirt flies up (much to the amusement of the boys) (GHSV F 114/16).

- We shouldn't have to wear such revealing clothes (GSHV F 156/16).

Girls are 'encouraged to relate to their bodies as objects that exist for the use and aesthetic pleasure of others, and to work on the improvement of their appearance. The body is to be held away from oneself, considered critically and judged by its attractiveness or unattractiveness' (Harris et al., 2000: 380). Many of the girls in our research talk about the expectations they feel regarding appearance and body image. They also link this focus on aspiring to 'the perfect image' to anorexia and mention the association of being thin with success:

- Girls I believe have a harder time at school because of the pressure to be like 'her' the perfect female role model, not only pretty but smart, popular and stress free. That never happens but everyone including me has some days when they don't care how much it takes but they WILL be like her and sometimes the female role model can go shove her head up her arse (GHS F 47/14).

- Girls got the hard end of the deal when god made us, he must have been really mad at Eve. Fair enough boys get a funny voice for a while, but us girls get stuck with periods every month. It's not fair, we seem to get depressed with our bodies more easily too. Two girls at my school are taking speed just so they won't feel hungry and can lose weight. They want to be perfect, but no-one is. But knowing this myself doesn't help me either. I still read magazines, go on diets and have crash diets where I don't eat too. All girls do (GHS F 54/15).

- Being around girls that are skinny, blonde, blue-eyed, etc can trigger the people and make them feel they have to go on a diet, even starve themselves to fit in (SSGS 112/16).

- How thin you are is associated with success and how big you are reflects low self-esteem and being unsuccessful … the weight loss issue concerns me greatly. One of my best friends has been in hospital for the past year with anorexia and I blame society and magazines like 'Dolly' and 'Girlfriend'. They are absolute hypocrites in the media world and they publish stories about how you shouldn't worry about how big you are and big is beautiful yet they persistently use absurdly skinny – almost anorexic looking models and many teenage girls are sucked in to thinking it is 'the perfect image' (CCHS F 89/16).

Thus, these girls highlight how being pretty and slim carries a particular social currency that confers a status femininity. Girls are rewarded for conforming to this so-called 'successful' traditional femininity by being positioned as sexually desirable by boys:

- The popular girls are often looked up to because they're gorgeous and they have the gorgeous boyfriends (GHSV F 104/16).

- Everybody tries to be the most popular and most beautiful and all the girls try to look good, lose weight (many girls diet) just so the boys like them and don't talk about them! Boys use the girls and make bets. Boys don't care about girls' personalities only the body and looks – and how loose they are. Girls go to school to impress boys (CCHS F 173/15).

A lot of anxiety informs the way many girls talk about the almost obsessive focus on body fashioning, with many mentioning eating disorders such as anorexia nervosa:

- All girls just wanna be stick skinny. In my grade, there is one girl who is getting a eating disorder and another girl who is already anorexic. This proves that girls (heaps of 'em) are still throwing out their lunches etc. just to stay skinny (CCHS F 145/16).

The issue of girls not being able to accept themselves if they fail to meet up to the normalised image of the ideal female body promoted by the media and their peers can have far-reaching consequences. Eating disorders, which are attributed to the internalisation of a negative female body and female self, are the extreme outcome (see Pallotta-Chiarolli, 1998; Harris et al., 2000).

A whole regime of self-regulatory practices involving girls' surveillance of their bodies emerged in their discourses about schooling and peer group relations. In the following, CCHS 88 borders and incorporates both traditional and transgressive femininity. For example, she finds herself 'fluctuating worse than the Channel 7 monsoon weather readings' as she negotiates the tensions and constructs of what it means to be a 'sensitive' traditional female and a 'thick-skinned stubborn mule' who hangs out with the drug-taking, partying 'shits-everyone-else crowd'. Ultimately, she can only classify herself according to a list of contradictions and complexities: 'schizophrenic, manic-depressive ... outspoken feministic bitchy ... egotistical, contradictory, confident yet insecure':

- Girls have to keep their image up; if their skirt is too long, you get pity, which is absolutely stupid. If you're not very good looking, you get disdain. If you're a 'popular' person, chances are you have to be a stereotypical superficial blonde bimbo ... I myself am not a 'popular' person by definition, meaning I don't hang with the huge either-clever-or-really stupid, doing drugs, wild party-animal, shits-everyone-else crowd, and I am so happy about that, not because I'm bitter (about this issue anyway) but because I love my friends and I couldn't stand being around the majority of these people anyway ... If you're overweight, you're insecure and you berate yourself everyday. If you're underweight, you worry about what other people think about your skinny arms etc. If you're too tall or short or hard-working or unattractive etc, it seems worse because of the other 200 people you see every day judging you on your appearance ... once I hit high school, it started fluctuating worse than the Channel 7 monsoon weather readings. At the moment I'm kind of stable, but about 2 days ago I was bouncing around everywhere and 2 weeks ago I was so down that I wished I didn't have a conscience and I had more willpower so I could go on a shooting spree at school and then kill myself, a la Port Arthur massacre (I've had this idea several times even before the American school shootings) which is scary, but as I mentioned, I don't have the confidence and lack of conscience and brainpower to become suicidal. Much better to become the homicidal, schizophrenic, manic-depressive psychic self-abhorring, outspoken feministic bitchy, self-absorbed, egotistical, contradictory, confident yet insecure, freakishly wonderful piece of crap that I am. From my views you can gather the effect that high school has on sensitive females, let alone the thick-skinned stubborn mules like me (CCHS F 88/15).

The *popular* transgressive girls, like the *popular* normative boys, are expected to be into drugs, drinking and wild parties. In our workshops with girls in schools, we are told of 'party games' initiated by boys that involve boys assigning to their girlfriends which girls to 'get it on' with in 'lesbian action' for the purpose of entertaining their boyfriends, and how boys will often threaten to 'dump' their girlfriends if the girls do not comply. Another party game is girls being assigned boys to give them head, blow jobs. Again, boys control the sexual proceedings and partnerings for the prime purpose of their pleasure. Thus, girls are expected to transgress traditional feminine constructs of heterosexual behaviour and sexual chastity, usually as long as it is constructed as part of normative boys' pleasure and controlled by boys themselves. Several girls in our research wrote about the combination of drinking, drugs and sex at parties and the role many girls were expected or wanted to perform in relation to boys and boyfriends:

- Girls are obsessed with sex and so the people who are not into that sort of thing are also singled out. Most girls find it really hard to have respect for themselves and other people and it really gets to me (SSGS 44/15).

- Only 'hot' girls will be invited to a party. I can see some of my friends seriously affected by this ... One other problem I see at school is friends who need to smoke/drink to be cool (SSGS 123/16).

- Sex is becoming more common and sometimes you need to keep up with 'picking up' at parties (SSGS 145/15).

- If you aren't willing to do something with a guy then you're not only shunned by the boys but the girls as well. I think it's unfair that girls think about boys all the time and talk about them all the time and the guys don't (SSGS 167/16).

PEER GROUP RELATIONS AND HIERARCHICAL FEMININITIES

Interestingly, the body features as a significant issue for girls in determining their popularity status in ways that were not evident in boys' discussions about their peer group relations and experiences of schooling. For many boys, as we have already illustrated, homophobia seemed to be at the heart of their regulatory practices governing the pecking order of masculinities at school. These gendered dimensions of identity formation are highlighted by the following girl:

- Girls and boys at the age of 16 are obsessed with their image. Boys seem to look at the sporting image, are they 'macho' or 'cool', and if they're not they may be faced with problems of being classed 'gay' unexpected. On the other hand, girls are obsessed with weight and do they look good. This is real comparing themselves with the media and what is in vogue at the time. If girls don't fit the image of being a good weight they are still accepted by the school yet not by themselves – this is different from the boys, as the boys may be able to accept themselves but aren't accepted by their friends. Weight and image is a frequent problem as I would lose count on my fingers the amount of girls who have had a weight problem (CCHS F 116/15).

However, the issue of body image was often seen as connected to the broader issues of gaining social acceptance and responding to the surveillance of girls by boys:

- As for being a girl at school I feel to get any attention from guys or some friends is to look good ... and be thin which is not right (RGHS F 29/16).

- The pressures for girls to be pretty and slim is a big issue as girls fear what boys say about them behind their backs ... boys tend to be insincere to girls, as they like them for their looks and how far they'll go with them, but not caring about what's inside (CCHS F 174/15).

- Appearance is one of the major factors as prettier girls or the ones that boys consider worthy to go out with tend to be the 'popular' ones. Nowadays boys have a major role in determining the social status of a girl. A girl a guy considers ugly would immediately be labelled 'unpopular'. The social hierarchy does not consist of the smart people, kind truthful people being at the top, but rather the bottom of the hierarchy, labelling these people as squids and/or sucks ... People are always told to judge a person by their personality, yet people still judge people on weight and looks. When girls talk about eligible guys the good-looking ones are always the top of the list, not the smart ones or nice ones (normally called nerds!). The effects of these are not good as many people suffer depression – school life is called 'the best years of childhood' whereas for many it is really a place of turmoil, where many cannot wait to go home and escape the realm of school (CCHS F 120/15).

Once again the detrimental consequences for girls' health and well-being of not measuring up to the social standards and ideals of embodied femininity dictated by the boys is highlighted by CCHS 120.

The following girl indicates that being in the popular group at the top of the peer group social ladder at school means that one escapes discrimination:

- It is harder in life for the people who aren't blessed with gorgeous features and attractive figure. Your face also has a part in that. Through my years I have been discriminated against for the above reasons, but since high school most of that has stopped because I am in the 'popular groups'. What does that say about peer influence and social hierarchy?? (CCHS F 135/15).

As another girl put it:

- It really all depends on what type of girl you are! (GHS F 25/15).

and where you are positioned and position yourself within the social hierarchy of peer group friendships and the oppositional duality of traditional and transgressive femininity (see Duncan, 2004).

However, the following girl, while highlighting the hierarchy and social status of girls' friendship groups at school, indicates that all girls, despite their peer group membership or affiliation, and their performance of a version of femininity, are faced with the same problem of 'looking good':

> - I'm the quiet one who sits in the corner and just listens to everyone else's gossip. Here's the way it is. First you've got the sporty groups. This consists mainly of guys with about 1/3 made up of girls. These girls are alright and nice. Then you have the squares. You know the ones who always get straight As and all the academic awards, mainly Asian (not being racist or anything just squares are usually Asians). These girls are nice too, nicer than the sports. Then there's the odd groups around who are a mixture of goth, grunge and surfy … They're pretty cool. I think I'm sorta one of them. Then of course you have the sluts!! The major smokers, the ones who have 3 inch thick make-up and the ones who are usually real bitches. They're into a lot of surfy brands and stuff and are always going out with someone. But that's just my point of view. It doesn't really matter. School for a girl is just being where you belong and doing whatever your group does but you still have to make sure you look good no matter what group you're in (GHS F 96/15).

What is interesting is that the classifications used by this girl draw attention to the hierarchical nature of peer group relations for girls at school. The particular role that sexuality plays in relegating to a certain group of girls a questionable and devalued status as 'sluts' (Tolman, 1999), which these girls then reclaim as transgressively *cool*, is emphasised. As Lees illustrated in her study, girls often put other girls down to differentiate themselves from the 'slags', and this, she claimed, was 'a way of protecting one's own reputation' (1993: 79). This relates once again to the issue of image, which many girls mentioned as a significant factor in the fashioning of their femininities, and highlights the precarious role for girls of maintaining a reputation that does not leave them open to ridicule and harassment, and yet does not mean being 'the quiet one who sits in the corner' who can be derided as 'frigid', a signifier of uncool, nerdy traditional femininity.

In adult cultures, male heterosexuality is still constructed as 'uncontrollable, forceful and autonomous' (Harris et al., 2000: 382), and this is taken on differentially by boys and girls in our study. Within this traditional gender regime, girls are required to take responsibility for containing the practices of male heterosexuality:

- I hate the way that in school if a boy fucks a girl, he's just a typical male but if a girl has sex she's the biggest slut on campus. If a boy does anything he's a hero, if a girl does she's a whore. It's really unfair (GHS F 72/15).

- You have to be careful of leading guys on (GHSV F 107/16).

Simultaneously, the construction of 'uncontrollable' male heterosexuality is manipulated by boys as justification for sexual coercion and an entitlement to 'pick up chicks' which translates into a 'masculinity confirming practice' that confers status (Renold, 2003):

- There are plenty of good-looking chicks to checkout (GHSV M 141/16).

- Being a boy is great, how many chicks that we can pick up (GHSV M 196/16).

According to the traditional gender hierarchy, female sexuality is:

> ... reactive, receptive and inferior. Women are supposed to attract men, and therefore derive sexual value and meaning from their physical attributes, while men are supposed to be the initiators of sexual encounters and the chief beneficiaries of the central heterosexual practice – penetration – especially in youth ... Young women learn that it is their sexual attractiveness to men that gives them legitimacy and value (Harris et al., 2000: 382).

Thus, according to simplistic binary constructions of girls in relation to their sexual expressions, they are either 'a good girl or a bad girl'. Harris et al. argue that transgressive girls endeavour to

> ... negotiate ways in which to enjoy heterosexual relationships in such terms that would not compromise their independence and agency [as] traditional normative prescriptions severely limit the ways in which alternative ideas of female maturity may be expressed. This may seriously undermine the agency of young women (2000: 386).

Tolman believes that the traditional/transgressive binary without young women being guided and supported in developing a transformative, balanced and assertive 'sexual subjectivity' is due to 'our consistent refusal to offer girls any guidance for acknowledging, negotiating, and integrating their own sexual desire' (2002: 3; see also Pallotta-Chiarolli, 1998). As she explains:

> By sexual subjectivity I mean a person's experience of herself as a sexual being, who feels entitled to sexual pleasure and sexual safety, who makes active sexual choices, and who has an identity as a sexual being. Teenage girls continue to be denied entitlement to their own sexuality, and girls who do defy the irrepressible double standard continue to do so at their own risk (2002: 5, 6–7).

Several girls who refuse to collude in masculinist 'good girl/bad girl' binary constructions reflect on the consequences of this refusal or question other girls' constructions of normative femininity:

- The shit the guys used to hang on me in my younger years made being an outgoing and kind of out there chick fucking suck! I used to get called 'the dyke that lost her bike'. It wasn't any of their business if I was a lesbian or not (though I'm not) but you know how boys are ... I got away from the shit and my marks picked up. Pity I've only got a year left of school actually being enjoyable and had 4 years of hell (GHSV F 211/16).

- Many of my peers are under the impression that their skirt being rolled up in winter (just below their butt cheeks) is attractive. All I can say to that is, 'Nice purple thighs girls, sure you're not cold?' (GHSV F 209/15).

Other girls critically assess the performances of other girls and problematise how their school structures endorse passive traditional feminine ways of relating to or being dependent upon male power and privilege:

- I have to deal with ... non-stop about boys. All my friends talk about boys, which I don't mind but talking about them more than half a day becomes tiring (SSGS 39/15).

- There is a pressure on us to move in the right social circles especially with boys. There is often pressure to have a boyfriend from another private boys' school (SSGS 26/15).

- It's bad how this school only socialises with our brother school. It's like they're planning our future husbands or something (SSGS 50/15).

INTERROGATING GENDER HIERARCHIES

Tolman writes about the young women who work toward balance and agency, which involves breaking the rules that dictate both traditional and transgressive femininities:

... these girls defy the very categories of good and bad, recognizing how this hierarchy separates girls from one another and diminishes and undermines them all. They are outspoken, irate, and defiant about their right to their own desire and pleasure in mutually acceptable circumstances ... They not only are aware of the double standard but also know what is wrong with it; and they not only see that it is unfair but also pinpoint what is unfair about it. [They are] engaging in a conscious refusal to comply with constrained constructions of who they can be and insisting on breaking rules they know to be unfair in order to be authentic and have integrity with themselves and others (2002: 151–52).

The following girl in our research is an example of Tolman's agentic young woman who is aware of how the gender 'hierarchy separates girls from one another and diminishes and undermines them all'. She is also aware of how the gender hierarchy within adolescent peer groups is reflective of the patriarchal inequities regarding gender and sexuality within the wider society:

- A few weeks back, my friends' boyfriends did a disgusting thing to my friend and the girls just stood back and laughed ... Ever since that night my friend and I have been social outcasts because those girls feel like it ... My Dad is Greek and he gives my brother more freedom than he does to me because he thinks the world is out to get me (SSGS 137/16/Greek/Croatian).

Here are three more young women who are engaging in 'a conscious refusal to comply with constrained constructions of who they can be' or, as Reay (2001) defines, 'transformative' femininity. These girls demonstrate the capacity to move beyond the confines and conformities of both traditional and transgressive femininities, which both support normative masculinist demands and behaviours. For example, GHSV 213 claims her sexual attraction to both boys and girls:

- I love school, I love both boys and girls, they're sexy! (GHSV F 213/16).

Likewise, SSGS 32 refuses to participate in traditional femininities organised around 'bitchiness about boys' and normative body image, and reclaims the label of 'geek' with pride:

- I'm proud to be a geek, free from petty bitching about boys and clothes ... sometimes the Britney Spears clones really piss me off (SSGS 32/15).

SSGS 17 refuses to participate in transgressive femininities organised around supposedly 'cool' practices of having a boyfriend, doing drugs and being part of 'unhealthy' social 'scenes' at the expense of valuing her education:

- I think girls have a lot of issues that can sometimes disrupt their school life (e.g. boyfriend, drugs etc) but I value my education too much to put myself in a situation that might jeopordise it. I know of girls that have trapped themselves in unhealthy scenes and this in turn has affected their attitude towards school (SSGS 17/15).

CONCLUSION

This chapter has drawn attention to the effects of body image and the fashioning of a particular sexualised femininity in relation to how many girls learn to regulate their desire. They endeavour to select a version of femininity to perform that will most effectively provide them with power and popularity, according to normative masculinist frameworks. These gendered norms which impact significantly on girls' experiences of schooling, with their emotional and psychological consequences, are erased within the current politicised context of a backlash against feminism in which boys emerge as the 'new disadvantaged' (Gilbert & Taylor, 1991; Lingard & Douglas, 1999; Foster et al., 2001; Martino et al., 2004). As Tolman argues:

> As long as the good-girl and bad-girl categories remain intact and as long as girls do not understand how this mechanism of keeping girls and women out of relationship with one another does not serve us, it will be nearly impossible for girls to trust one another ... They need to see how our conceptions of male and female sexuality are social constructions that produce privilege and oppression. The importance of developing this knowledge in the context of supportive, trustworthy relationships cannot be underestimated (2002: 195–96, 199).

Likewise, Reay concludes in her study, 'The contemporary orthodoxy that girls are doing better than boys masks the complex messiness of gender relations in which, despite [some] girls' better educational attainment ... the prevalent view is still that it's better being a boy' (2001: 164).

This raises important issues about the need to consider the influences and factors impacting on the educational and social well-being of both boys and girls in schools (see Lingard, Martino, Mills & Bahr, 2003). For example, Tolman challenges the masculinist justification of the 'obsessive surveillance of the sexual behavior of adolescent girls' in educational policy:

> To act upon one's own sexual feelings and desire is still, for girls, to invite the risk of being labelled as a 'bad' girl, a girl who deserves any consequences she suffers, a girl who loses her eligibility for social and legal protections against sexual harm ...If these risks were our deepest concerns, we would be pouring funds into effective, accessible forms of birth control and protection against diseases, providing comprehensive sexuality education, widely disseminating information on masturbation and mutual masturbation as the safest forms of sexual exploration, declaring 'zero tolerance' for sexual violence or the threat of it and for homophobia (2002: 12–13).

This is exemplified by the following student who claims that

- Many of my friends are having sex. Some of them are stupid enough to believe that they won't get pregnant even though they have unprotected sex every weekend with different people each time. Sluts (SSGS 25/15).

As SSGS 25 illustrates, it is her female friends who are judged for having unprotected sex, and this is indicative of a wider educational and societal discourse that constructs adolescent boys as driven by 'intense sexual desire' which is driven by 'a natural and normal part of male adolescence and male sexuality' (Tolman, 2002: 12–13):

> A gendered perspective on adolescent sexuality offers more explanation for what is behind the urgency of resisting girls' sexual desire: Girls' lack of desire serves as the necessary linchpin in how adolescent sexuality is organised and managed [by adults] ... Our impulse to keep girls safe by keeping them under control seems so necessary that the cost of denying them the right to live fully in their own bodies appears unavoidable (Tolman, 2002: 12–13, 15).

Thus, Tolman supports Fine's (1988) work on 'the missing discourse of desire', which pointed out nearly twenty years ago 'our insistence on defining female adolescent sexuality only in terms of disease, victimization, and morality and our avoidance of girls' own feelings of sexual desire and pleasure' (Tolman, 2002: 14). The two responses below from a girl and a boy in the same school exemplify this. While the girl is aware of how she is judged negatively for any sign of sexual desire and expression, the boy is able to enthusiastically claim that being able to find sexual partners at school is the best thing about going to school:

- It's ok being a girl at school except when we have casual clothes days and get compared to the tarts (GHSV F 74/16).

- I get lots of free sex (GHSV M 98/16).

Tolman believes we need to have 'a different conversation altogether', one that says that:

> Girls live and grow up in bodies that are capable of strong sexual feelings ... teenage girls' sexual desire is important and life sustaining; that girls' desire provides crucial information about the relational world in which they live; that the societal obstacles to girls' and women's ability to feel and act on their own desire should come under scrutiny rather than simply be feared; that girls and women are entitled to have sexual subjectivity, rather than simply to be sexual objects (2002: 16).

BEING A GIRL

AIM • To develop a deep understanding about the impact of femininity on girls' lives at school

NORMALISATION

Many girls engage in a form of self-policing that involves a conscious fashioning of appearance, body weight and body image. The desire for a particular sort of slim body and appearance impacts significantly on girls' lives at school.

There are hierarchies of femininity or certain classifications of girls. This pecking order is based on a notion of being popular that involves body image, weight and looks.

SEXUALITY

Challenging or transgressing traditional femininity can lead to girls' sexuality being policed in problematic ways.

Girls still have to tread a fine line between being perceived as sexually promiscuous and, hence, a 'whore' or as a virgin with its connotations of being frigid and 'tight'.

For many girls, boys play a major role in the policing of their sexuality. This involves girls being exposed to labelling and harassment as 'dykes, sluts and butch'.

REJECTING HIERARCHICAL AND 'COOL' FEMININITIES

Many girls interrogate what it means to be cool and the social hierarchy it confers. They question the popularity stakes of having a boyfriend and being a part of unhealthy social scenes.

DISCUSSION FORUM

THEME 1 • **GIRLS' BODIES**

What kinds of body issues do these girls draw our attention to? How would these issues impact upon their ability to participate effectively in learning? How are these issues being addressed in the curriculum, official student welfare and pastoral care policies at your school?

- I think going through puberty is harder for girls ... Hairy legs are a bit of a stress in summer uniform! It's also hard as everybody develops at different stages ... boys would worry about a lack of body hair while girls would worry about too much. Height would be more of an issue with boys, while attractiveness and weight would be a bigger worry for girls. Boys don't have to worry about swimming lessons when they have their 'friend' and girls would not have to worry about bodily fluids like boys (SSGS 60/15).

- It's hard at lunch times when everyone eats junk and are thin and I'm sitting with one bloody pear just so I can feel better about myself (SSGS 131/16).

- It's OK being a girl at school because you are all treated the same. Yet the type of issue you have to deal with being a girl is looking your best, not being too fat, that is the biggest issue your weight and always thinking you are too fat (CCHS F 138/15).

- People seem to judge you by how you look, making up their minds in 5 seconds about whether you would be worth talking to or not. With this kind of pressure, it is hard not to conform to the 'accepted' image (SSGS 97/16).

THEME 2 • GIRLS' SOCIAL LIFE OUTSIDE OF SCHOOL

What social practices or expectations influence girls' behaviour outside of school? How do these behaviours relate to or impact on girls' experiences at school? How are schools addressing these social issues in the curriculum, official student welfare and pastoral care policies?

- Our group is also quite boy-obsessed and already most of them have done things which I really think are too mature for them. However mostly they're conforming to the idea that being cool and popular results from being sexually advanced and having boyfriends … girls suffer pressure to do things with boys (SSGS 166/16).

- The behaviour at parties often involves smoking and excessive drinking … often I think it is just the influence of the Anglo-Saxon culture … it's socially acceptable behaviour. I was heartbroken a couple of weeks ago when I witnessed alcohol induced sex that was immediately regretted … I hate it when beer funnels are brought to parties (SSGS 128/16/Italian).

- Boyfriends and whether you have them and how far you've gone with them comes into the category of peer pressure (SSGS 130/16).

- There are problems at school dealing with people's outside lifestyles eg girls who have boyfriends and incidences that occur outside school life. It affects how people act out at school through the pressure of peers forcing people to conform to their 'partying' ways (SSGS 53/15).

- I feel that girls have a lot more issues to deal with because not one girl I know is ever happy with the way they act, look or speak or think and that is sad (CCHS F 169/16).

THEME 3 • THE INFLUENCE OF BOYS

What do these girls' comments reveal about the power of boys to dictate girls' self-esteem, appearance and sexual behaviour? How are these issues being addressed at your school? Are these gendered power relations specifically named and addressed within sexual harassment policies and health and personal development?

- I think it's good that our PE lessons are our only single sex class, because it means that the girls don't have to worry about what the guys think of them. Other girls don't care. That's one of the pressures in the school, that girls place too much emphasis and value on being attractive. Even just with simple things like the way we do our hair and how we wear our uniform. I think there is a lot more pressure like this placed on girls than there is on boys (CCH5 F 160/15).

- Being a girl at school is hard because you have to matter what you look like. If you're too fat or too short or too ugly you have to try and improve yourself for the sake of boys' pleasure. Girls have to deal with their periods and period pains at school and boys have to deal with none of that, just being immature little pricks. My other problem is getting teased by people because I'm bigger than them (GHS F 92/15).

- Being a girl at school can be hard. Boys judge you from your looks, chest and figure. I think that girls are categorised into groups more than what boys are. You have to fit into other people's expectations (GHS F 53/15).

- Girls have to deal with so much especially if you want to be accepted by boys. You're either a cool chick or not and if you don't have a hot body guys just block you out. It's annoying how guys like the dumb girls and guys are so dumb all the time (GHSV F 110/16).

- Some people think that you need alcohol to have fun … Some girls feel pressure to do stuff with guys and in a way, sometimes it is sad to see that some girls don't really care about their bodies or don't have much integrity in relation to guys (SSGS 144/16).

5

BOYS HARASSING GIRLS IN SCHOOL: 'Girls have it harder cos they have to deal with guys'

- Boys receive no sort of trouble from girls (normally) yet girls cop a lot (CCHS M 47/17).

IN THIS CHAPTER YOU WILL:

- learn more about boys' harassment of girls at school;
- develop a better understanding about the extent to which certain forms of harassment are gendered and implicated in asserting masculine superiority;
- engage in a Professional Development session using girls' voices to build knowledge about the impact of gender-based harassment on their lives.

INTRODUCTION

For many girls, life at school was characterised by harassment, often perpetuated by boys and directed at either calling into question their sexual reputation or specifically targeting their appearance and bodies. These sexist practices, which continue to persist, present the flip side to the success that girls have supposedly achieved at the expense of boys (Forster et al., 2001). While some important gains have been made for girls educationally, what remains unaltered is the sex-based harassment by boys of girls and those marginalised boys who do not measure up to the dictates of hegemonic heterosexual masculinity (Frank, 1987). There are issues related to the psychological and emotional well-being of both girls and subordinated boys that must continue to be the focus of attention in the formulation of policies at the local and national level which draw attention to the gendered and sex-based dimensions of bullying. Significantly, this is omitted from the report on the parliamentary inquiry into boys' education (House of Representatives Standing Committee, 2002).

Underlying much of the school-based harassment and bullying is an unnamed gender system built on the denigration and devaluation of the feminine as exemplified in the following girl's statement:

- Boys sometimes say you're a chick, you can't do that, but really you can (GHSV F 180/16).

What is also of note here is the girl's resistance to such a sexist positioning and construction of women. However, the question arises: to what extent are schools erasing or no longer engaging with such basic inequities due to a backlash construction of political correctness that makes it 'uncool' to raise such a concern? When the dominant neo-conservative political system declares that men and boys are now the victims, how do we construct spaces to interrogate the persistence of oppressive gender hierarchies? Our position, based on the research with young people documented in this book, calls for a need and a commitment to giving voice to girls and those marginalised boys in schools who are subjected to the very systems of hegemonic male power and compulsory heterosexuality that lead to harassment, suffering and other social behaviours detrimental to the health and well-being of all citizens. To what extent are schools actively questioning these gender regimes and to what extent are they perpetrating them? And ultimately, how are the girls and marginalised boys who are endeavouring to resist such gender-based hierarchies and harassment supported and affirmed by the school?

BOYS' SEX-BASED HARASSMENT AND POLICING OF GIRLS' SEXUALITY

Boys emerged as a definite problem for girls in our research. Their sexist, misogynist and femiphobic behaviour and practices contributed in significant ways to impacting detrimentally on the quality of girls' lives and self-esteem at school (see Kenway et al., 1997; Pallotta-Chiarolli, 1998). Lees, in fact, claims that:

> British researchers too have found between the ages of thirteen and sixteen some girls in school lose confidence, become more passive, contribute less in class and become less eager to participate ... (1993:29).

Our research, conducted a decade later, would tend to support the view that boys' sexist and harassing behaviours still play a significant role in influencing girls' social practices and fashioning of their femininities, which then impact on their self-esteem. Many girls across all schools we surveyed wrote about boys' harassing behaviours. The following girls highlight the impact emotionally and psychologically of boys at school:

- Girls have it harder cos they have to deal with guys ... sexism is alive! (GHSV F 13/16).

- The biggest thing at school I think that depresses me are the boys. I think I've learnt from school that boys don't always say things they mean and if they do say it they're either drunk or maybe there's an odd chance they could be true. Girls have to deal with boys at school and I think it would have to be a big part of school. Some of my friends have even considered suicide because of things like boys (GHS F 113/15).

The above student, while acknowledging the severity of boys' sex-based harassment on girls' emotional well-being, slips into a traditional feminine mode of justifying or excusing boys' abusive behaviour as being unintentional or as a result of the influence of alcohol. She appears to be suggesting that they may not be fully responsible for their harassing behaviours. This calls into question the kinds of normative essentialist or biological constructions of masculinity within the wider social culture that girls resort to applying in order to explain or account for boys' actions and behaviour (Harris et al., 2000; Reay, 2001; Tolman, 2002).

Most girls were quite explicit about the sex-based harassment and policing of their sexuality perpetuated by boys. In fact, as we have discussed in the previous chapter, Lees demonstrates:

> ... how girls lose confidence because their identity rests to such an extent on their sexual reputation, which is precarious and crucial to them (1993: 29).

In order to counteract such policing and sexual labelling by boys, girls such as the following adopt strategies of self-regulation and self-surveillance in order to deflect boys' harassment:

> - Guys give you a lot of shit, but you have to get over it and learn not to let them upset you ... Guys used to hassle me but now I'm getting along with them. Just a thing to remember, don't be too slutty in front of them otherwise they won't respect you, that is what I have learnt in the past year (RGHS F 19/16).
>
> - Being a girl is pretty hard cause you always look great to impress the guy or you get called a dirty scrag or you can be called a slut for having sex with a guy even if he was your boyfriend etc. (RGHS F 20/16).

Thus, girls find themselves attempting to negotiate a midpoint between traditional and transgressive performances of the sexual self that will best avoid boys' abuse and yet best serve their own sexual desires. In fact, Lees argues that:

> Girls walk a narrow line: they must not be seen as too tight, nor as too loose. Girls are preoccupied in their talk with sexuality, and in particular with the injustice of the way they are treated by boys. Defining girls in terms of sexuality rather than their attributes and potentialities is a crucial mechanism of ensuring their subordination to boys (1993: 29).

In a review of the literature and research on adolescent girls and their sexual behaviours and relationships, Tolman found:

> ... 'overwhelming documentation' of inequalities of power in sexual relationships and encounters that are determined by boys' interests, needs, and desires ... [and] within a framework of social constraints, including (a) male pressure that can be as intense as male violence; (b) passive femininity; (c) girls' sense of responsibility for male sexuality; and (d) a 'missing discourse of desire' as described by Michelle Fine (1988) ... young women have to be prepared to lose valued social relationships in order to assert control over their sexuality (1999: 235).

This is confirmed by what the following girls have to say about boys at school:

- Girls have to worry about their 'image' – if she is beautiful then she must be a 'slut'. Boys are 'hurrayed' upon if they sleep with girls and girls are 'frowned' upon if they sleep with boys (CCHS F 105/15).

- In my year especially, the boys are very persuasive when it comes to girls. They ALWAYS have the upper hand and congregate in groups to intimidate. Girls then feel they have to live up to the expectations and standards of the 'guys' and become fake. Their personality isn't their real personality and they do anything only for a guy's approval. Personally I find it PATHETIC! And I let them know it. I can only because I'm in the 'POPULAR' group but someone who spends their lunch times in the library or computer room could never, as they would face embarrassment and harassment ... Girls

> live up to the expectation of the 'boys group'. It's all
> about doing something only if it's cool and the others
> will approve of it and condone it. That's all that seems
> to matter!! ... I also get sick of how guys talk about
> girls in sexual ways and judge their personality on their
> bra size!! It's demeaning and it affects girls. They will
> do anything a guy says, just so they won't be thought
> of as a 'tight-ass'. That's what school life to me
> involves! (CCHS F 112/15).

As CCHS 105 indicates, the familiar sexist practice still persists where a boy's reputation is enhanced by having sex, while that of a girl's is called into question. The point made by CCHS 112 regarding boys' power to intimidate is also important because it relates to how boys establish certain power bases in peer group situations and then use this power in intimidatory ways to police girls' sexuality and femininities. Having a girlfriend and being a boyfriend is 'an overt "compulsory" signifier for the public affirmation of a boy's heterosexuality, and a further performative signifier of their hegemonic masculinity' (Renold, 2003: 181). Renold discusses how boys 'define and produce their heterosexualities through various public projections of (hetero)sexual fantasies, imagined (hetero)sexual futures, misogynistic objectifications of girls and women, and homophobic/anti-gay performances towards boys and sexualised forms of harassment towards girls' (2003: 179).

ASSERTING MASCULINE SUPERIORITY

Interestingly, the increasing refusal of some girls to occupy 'passive sexual subject positions' in boyfriend/girlfriend relationships has been found to mean that the boys display their heterosexual masculine superiority through other ways such as 'the sexual objectification of girls and women; ... sexualising classroom talk; ... symbolic sexual gestures; sexual swear words; physical sexual harassment; and homophobic discourses' (Renold, 2003: 184). The following girls actually highlight how boys' harassment of girls is linked to asserting their superiority which, in turn, is linked to fashioning a cool masculinity in peer group situations:

- Most guys give the girls crap about how we as girls look, because it's 'cool', it's 'fun' and it impresses their mates. If you were to be locked away with them in a room, they would be the most sweetest, most kindest person (creature?) you could ever have come across and I think it's really dumb (pathetic?), how they have to use these masks to keep their 'supreme' title and carry it out till the end ... (CCHS F 96/15).

- The guys are mostly nice but those higher on the social ladder tease girls that are not as popular or attractive as others. The teasing is continuous and everyone learns to handle it ... There is always a pressure to be popular and some girls endeavor to get into the popular group, dieting etc in a chance to be popular and get the guys they want (CCHS F 121/15).

CCHS 121 draws attention to how the popular boys are the ones who do the teasing and suggest that this is a means of subordinating those girls who do not measure up to their standards of acceptable femininity. Furthermore, what is highlighted by such a response is that boys' harassing behaviours are a means by which they are able to establish and maintain their powerful position at the top of the social ladder of peer group relations at school consisting of a pecking order of masculinities and femininities. In fact, many girls talked about how boys teased and ridiculed them on the basis of their appearance, which was once again seen as linked to boys asserting masculine power through sexist practices of denigrating girls. However, the denigration of girls is a strategy utilised by boys to establish their status as certain sorts of powerful boys. Interestingly, girls often interrogated this behaviour and identified boys' anxieties over their own positioning within masculinist hierarchies as driving their harassment of girls:

- Most of the boys at our school think they are superior to everyone else and they think they can have fixed images of what girls should look like and if you don't fit this image then you get called moles and picked on for any physical appearance that is different.

I think they are doing this to compensate for them not being Gods themselves. The issues boys have to deal with are feeling they have to fit a certain image and if they don't they will be picked on (CCHS F 159/15).

BOYS' HOMOPHOBIC HARASSMENT OF GIRLS

This denigration and policing of girls' femininities by boys also involved homophobic harassment, with the latter often labelling certain girls 'lesbian' (Ferfolja, 1998; Robinson, 1996):

- Somehow I threaten people, mainly guys. I get teased because I dress weird and if I want to dance I dance, I want to do star jump I do etc. I don't really care what others think so they tease. You could say I go looking for it, with the might take it or leave it attitude, but it's hard to survive, it's like school the final frontier, hehe. And I have friends that are also considered weird, they are my close group of friends. I get 'lesbian' a LOT. I am not but I do have 2 friends that are, and what's the big deal! The teasing is not stupid sing song rhymes or anything, it's embarrassing questions asked loudly around a big group of people which made me shy and uncomfortable. 'Are you and your sister lesbians?'. What's that? I don't ask them if they sleep with their sister let alone sibling of the same sex – how rude is that (CCHS F 98/15).

- I copped a lot of flack because of the abbreviation of my name I like to be called because it is a boy's name (traditionally). It was mainly guys that called me these things, it drove me to a self-inflicting state but I got help from a student program designed to help kids with problems like mine. In Year 9, I got teased HEAPS and I was called a lesbian. Only heavily teased girls in our grade get stuff like that spread about them. I guess I got picked – lucky me (CCHS F 119/15).

This girl's comment that 'only heavily teased girls' are called lesbians highlights how, according to the dictates of compulsory heterosexuality governing these boys' behaviours, to be considered or labelled a lesbian is to position a girl at the lowest rung of the social ladder. Thus, there appears to be a hierarchy of harassment whereby homophobic harassment of both boys and girls is constructed as the worst form of denigration. What is also of interest is that very few girls identified homophobic harassment as a hierarchical ranking strategy within their peer groups in the same way as boys do. It appears that boys use homophobia to both police other boys' masculinity and girls who do not conform to the masculinist constructions of traditional femininities. This also extends to those girls who transgress these traditional feminine norms but only if they are not engaging in heterosexual relationships on boys' terms. The impact of this kind of harassment can be very detrimental to lesbian and bisexual girls, as their desire comes to be seen as:

> ... a source of danger and threat to their relationships with female friends, parents, and others ... [and] dealing with cultural norms of heterosexuality made it very hard to stay connected with their desire for girls and to stay clear about their identity (Tolman, 1999: 241).

This kind of harassing behaviour was often dismissed and trivialised by some girls as a manifestation of boys' immaturity:

- I get a lot of crap from immature guys, they call me bitch and a lot of other stuff I can't write but it doesn't bother me ... (CCHS F 113/15).

However, for the most part, boys' harassing and 'immature' behaviour was not seen as harmless or something that many girls could easily dismiss in this way. It was reported as having major consequences socially for many girls in its capacity to affect significantly the quality of their lives at school:

- There are some people who are intent on making your school life hell. These are mostly boys. Most of the time they're alright, when they're on their own, but when they

> hang around in big groups of 10 or 20 people, they apparently feel like they have a superiority over everybody else, and it can be intimidating. They constantly tease people who may be on the big side, or people who are quiet (God knows why) or people who are from another country etc. They seem to get their jollies out of this kind of behaviour. They are only kind to the 'popular' girls or the 'we think we're cool' girls. These tend to be the snobbish girls who look down on you like you're a piece of lint on their stockings. They think that everyone likes them when really, all the 'normal' people hate their guts. These boys and girls are usually the ones who are out on Friday nights getting high on drugs and alcohol. And then they brag about them! Gee, I'd really like to be like that! Back to the boys. They're mean to people who go to the library to study at lunch times! They think, 'Oh we're so cool, we don't study'. Let me ask something. In the end what's going to be more important at university or TAFE? – the person who did well, but maybe weren't so 'popular' or the person who was 'popular' but did crap all at school? (CCHS F 149/15).

This narrative highlights how the negotiation of high status masculinities and femininities is situated within a context of particular power relations that are maintained through regimes of social practices subscribed to by both the *popular* girls and boys at school. However, what needs to be emphasised is that the boys tended to police the girls' femininities in ways that were not available to girls in terms of dictating boys' practices of masculinity. In fact, the dominant cool boys tended to be the power brokers in the subordination and policing of both girls and non-hegemonic boys (see Collins et al., 1996; Tolman, 1999).

However, many girls indicated that boys were not the only perpetrators of such forms of harassment and policing (see Lees, 1993). As Hey points out in her research with girls:

> The compulsion to sort out what it meant to be acceptably feminine was intense. It was driven by the demands of the boys and the competitive relations between 'different' girls as well … (1997: 106).

Interestingly in the single-sex school, while boys were not physically present, they still emerged as a significant absence in their capacity to dictate the norms governing the harassment and hierarchical positioning between girls. In short, girls' relationships with boys outside school often became the impetus for the nature of the 'bitchiness' between girls and was incisive in disturbing and destabilising girls' friendship bonds:

- Most of the problems at school come from friendship groups, and even then the fights are caused by boys whether it be what has happened at a party when someone likes/doesn't like etc. ... Many girls getting jealous over guys mainly like I'm always getting jealous of my friends with guys because they always get them but I don't let it bother me even though my friends only talk about boys boys boys (SSGS 110/16).

- One girl and I are fighting and it is because my boyfriend did something not too cool and she feels it's my fault and is taking it out on me. That causes tension within the group. (SSGS 124/16).

CONCLUSION

Regardless of the structure of the school, co-educational or single sex, our research draws attention to the pervasive and intensified forms of sex-based harassment directed at girls and driven by boys. What does not appear to have changed is the extent to which girls still feel compelled to police their femininities and sexualities in masculinist terms framed by the dictates of the 'Madonna/whore' binary. In addition, there appears to be a hierarchy of harassment perpetrated by a certain group of hegemonic or 'cool' boys that is directed at other marginalised boys and those girls who transgress masculinist constructions of femininity. One of the significant gendered dimensions of the nature of this harassment was the use of homophobia by boys to police both non-normative boys and girls in ways that were not evident in the negotiation and establishment of hierarchies amongst girls.

Finally, what also appeared in the data was that even when boys were not present, their all-encompassing gaze and surveillance still emerged as significant in determining the social and emotional dynamics for girls in their friendship groups and social hierarchies. Hence, the question that begs to be asked is: why do public debates about 'the boy problem' and the report on the parliamentary inquiry into boys' education remain silent on these issues? Why are school-based policies failing to address the evidence that young people provide us with about their everyday realities regarding harassment and the role of hegemonic masculinity as a driving force in perpetuating oppressive gender-based hierarchies? Given the call for more male role models in schools, what questions are being asked about the role of male teachers in counteracting a system of gender-based harassment that is perpetrated by boys who subscribe to hegemonic masculinist power structures?

BOYS HARASSING GIRLS IN SCHOOL

AIM • To develop a deep understanding about boys' harassment of girls at school

BOYS' SEX-BASED HARASSMENT OF GIRLS

This involves policing girls' sexuality through the Madonna/whore binary.

At the heart of this sexist harassment is the need for boys to assert their masculine superiority, which involves displaying their heterosexuality.

The popular or the 'cool' boys are often the perpetrators of sex-based harassment against girls.

DISCUSSION FORUM

THEME 1 • **BOYS HARASSING GIRLS**

What forms of harassment do the girls identify? How are these issues being addressed at the school policy level?

- You have to deal with boys teasing you (GHSV F 200/16).

- You sometimes get hit by balls when boys are playing ... And boys are sometimes jerks (GHSV F 145/15).

- You're surrounded by annoying boys (GHSV F 103/16).

- If you are a girl and have a lot of female friends, the guys will call you a lesbian, but we can deal with that. It's really hard, if you are a girl to stand up for another person against guys ... The insults get really personal, even down to saying one guy's mum is a whore because she has 7 kids (CCHS F 92/15).

THEME 2 • **QUESTIONING THE 'SLUT/STUD' DICHOTOMY**

How are girls constrained by the label 'slut'? How is this being addressed explicitly in student welfare policies and curriculum at your school?

- I am a girl and I have a lot of male friends. Immediately I am classed as a slut and this makes it hard for me to make friends because of this name. Guys think 'slut ... I'll get lucky tonight' so they immediately come to me. It's hard to deal with this because everyone finds out and hassles me at school. The hard thing for me to understand is that when girls have sex they are called a 'slut' but when guys have sex everyone thinks they are a hero. This is wrong and it hurts me to think that the world is coming to this conclusion (RGHS F 21/16).

- Being a girl at school is hard sometimes like it's so easy to get a bad name with people especially guys, you know, being called a slut (GHS F 82/15).

- Being a girl at school is not easy because if you don't look nice you get teased and if you look too nice you get called a slut and boys you don't like run after you (GHS F 103/15).

THEME 2 • BOYS IN GIRLS' FRIENDSHIPS WITH EACH OTHER

How do girls' relationships with boys outside school impact on their friendships with other girls inside school?

- Girls have to sometimes deal with the uncomfortable feeling that guys may not like them and therefore their friends might not include them on the weekend. This then causes a problem when people at school are talking about what happened at the party or what will happen that weekend coming up and the person can feel left out and hurt (SSGS 100/16).

- Recently the group of friends I've been in has had a falling out due to boys and their immaturity. The boys haven't copped anything but all the girls have been bitching. Most times now when I'm with my friends I feel excluded and left out. I was abused by guys that were my friends, and all the people that I thought were my friends turned against me (SSGS 103/16).

6

'BULLY BOYS' AND 'BITCH BARBIES': Gender-based harassment in schools

- Girls get picked on or bullied for different reasons than boys. This is because it is more important for girls to look 'normal'. They don't want to be called 'fat', 'ugly' or a 'slut'. Boys don't worry as much about their weight etc ... Most girls don't bully other girls to their faces unless they are in a fight with that person. Boys, on the other hand, tend to bully each other constantly about the way they look etc. They are more open with their bullying and don't talk about people behind their back as much as girls do ... (CCHS F 100/15).

IN THIS CHAPTER YOU WILL:

- learn more about the gendered dimensions of harassment for boys and girls at school;
- develop a deeper understanding of the effects of bullying on both boys and girls at school;
- engage in a Professional Development session using girls' and boys' voices to investigate the consequences of bullying.

INTRODUCTION

The gendered dimensions of harassment and bullying at school are summarised effectively by the young woman above and were a strong focus in survey responses. As discussed in previous chapters, 'bitchiness' poses a major problem for girls in their social relationships with one another at school. Many talk at length about the social pressures that resulted from 'bitchiness' as a specific form of gender-based harassment amongst girls used to maintain and establish certain power relations (see Lees, 1993; Hey, 1997; Pallotta-Chiarolli, 1998; Tanenbaum, 2002). Also discussed in previous chapters and not adequately acknowledged in backlash educational debates is 'bitchiness' as a symptom or consequence of establishing or maintaining a hierarchy of girls in relation to the 'cool' or popular boys. Thus, bitchiness often occurs because of jealousy or rivalry in relation to boys.

BITCHINESS AND EXCLUSIONARY PRACTICES OF FEMININITY

In this chapter, we focus specifically on students' perceptions of the gendered dimensions of harassment and bullying: 'bully boys and bitch Barbies' – which was often expressed in binary terms with girls' bitchiness being set against boys' bullying or physical fighting:

- Guys have to deal with physical violence and girls deal with bitching (SSBS 23/16).

- Girls have to deal with bitchiness; boyz haf to deel with machoness ... (RGHS F 18/15).

- Through bitchiness, I have lost friends. (Other females or ex-friends have started trouble for me). I have put up with a lot of hassles, but I have been helped out by school counsellor, the principal and the deputy principals. I have tried not to let the bitchiness bring my grades down but unfortunately for me my parents, teachers and I have all noticed that my grades have dropped and we all know that this has been caused by stress. I am in high classes but since I started to get hassled I have been dropped down two classes ... I am hoping that soon the troublemakers will realise that they have made me suffer and hopefully they will realise that they had enough fun and are now bored with hassling me (hopefully) (RGHS F 28/14).

Thus bitchiness features as a significant form of harassment in girls' lives and is linked to issues of 'coolness', popularity and competition amongst girls and often in relation to boys (see Duncan, 2004). In her study of 'bitching' or what are also referred to as 'catfights', Tanenbaum draws direct links to dominant constructions of masculinity and femininity and their implications for how boys and girls are 'permitted' to display anger or aggression:

> While boys are given permission to punch and kick to express negative feelings, girls are taught to avoid direct conflict ... Many girls mastered the machinations of indirect aggression: they know, even at a young age, that they are supposed to appear good and demure and deferential, not overtly aggressive ... Exclusion is one of the most sinister forms of aggression and one of the most popular among young girls ... Girls, who aren't supposed to get into rough-and-tumble fights, instead form hate clubs (2002: 43, 45–46).

This is further substantiated by the following girls:

- I get left out a lot by my friends, although I sit in a group, no-one really talks to me ... during class when it's one on one with my friends, they are really nice and we talk for ages about everything you can possibly think of, but when we get back to the rest of the group, they walk off, ignore me and talk about people I don't know or things they have done without me. I feel sad about being left out, if you don't have connection and don't work to act 'cool' no-one really wants to talk to you or know you ... bitching and gossiping are the worst things in the world to have to deal with (SSGS 46/14).

- I find that girls can hurt you emotionally which takes longer to heal (SSGS 100/16).

Tanenbaum also directly relates 'bitching' between girls to gendered hierarchies:

> Many women compete over things they think men value, such as looking sexy ... Society still conditions girls and women to believe they are inferior to boys and men ... The most dangerous outcome of this is self-hatred: girls and women disparage themselves and disassociate from other females ... male approval is more significant than female approval (2002: 29–30).

Girls in the workshops Maria has conducted with schools have used the term 'bitch Barbies' to define those who deliberately harass other girls based on their supposed superiority due to combinations of wealth, body image, Anglo-Australian backgrounds, and popularity with boys. Sometimes, the school's own class status is seen by some girls to perpetuate the dominance of wealthy, white, thin, blonde 'bitch Barbies':

- I feel that the atmosphere is very much based on one's wealth and I hate that ... My family has had to work hard, just like I do, and some girls think they are so hard done by just because they have to eat bread that is one day old. I also don't like the racism here ... even my friends have been racist ... I hate the way the majority of girls have the easy road because they have money (SSGS 13/15/Indian-Italian).

- This school is really judgmental most of the times coz most of the girls are rich families whose daddys buy them anything they want, because of this the girls think they're better than everyone else (SSGS 37/15).

- Girls worry more about physical appearance eg being fat, having the right shoes, hair, etc. If you do one thing wrong you'll end up getting backstabbed and then become a LOSER! (GHSV F 118/16).

The following are examples of how some girls construct hierarchies among themselves in response to masculinist definitions and hierarchies from the most desired or 'normal' girl to the least desired or most 'abnormal':

- The guys at my school are not very kind to me and most of the time I don't even utter one word to them and they will be mean to me. Most of the time I don't even associate with them and just from false rumours and their deluded behaviour they think they can say and do whatever they want. Girls have to deal with a lot at school, they feel they have to compete with each other at times and I find it sad because especially the popular girls have these egocentric attitudes which revolts me, they think they are the best thing God created and as soon as they realise they are not, they start bawling their eyes out, it's so sick! And the worst thing is the majority of the girls in this school are so self-destructive and they lie to themselves when they say they are not. All of them have this major issue of sex and that's what they mostly want to do, why do they go to school if sex is the only thing in their minds? ... I am in a small minority who want to have fun and succeed as well (CCHS F 104/16).

- Girls have to deal with growing up in front of everyone and have a lot of pressure to 'fit in' with other girls. A lot of boys have to deal with peer pressure and to face a lot of bullies and be a part of fights. It is more common for girls to be given a 'bad' name and to have rumours spread about them than boys. You have problems throughout high school with girls that think they're better than you and can push you around but you end up realising that you're the better person because they dropped out of school at Year 10 to work full time at [fast food takeaway] (GHS F 114/15).

These 'sensible' girls (Hey et al., 2001), or 'balanced bods', however, appear to be distancing themselves from both the 'immaturity' of the boys and the destructive 'bitchiness' of the girls in favour of investing in academic success at school, which they see as affording them greater post-school opportunities (see Francis, 2000). However, while Francis found that girls had higher levels of motivation and achievement than boys at school, she indicated that a possible explanation for this:

> ... might be a feeling that they need to do better than boys in order to compete with them on even terms in the workplace ... these girls and boys believed that where a woman and a man were equally able the man would be more likely to be selected for employment or promotion (2000: 85).

This is supported by Rees (1999) who claims that boys are more likely to be given apprenticeships and to find work in the industrial sector (see also Collins et al., 2000).

FIGHTING MASCULINITIES

Many girls explicitly related 'bitching' to 'fitting in' and to the set standards or norms governing how they are expected to behave. Informing many of these responses are gendered dichotomies to explain the differential social practices of boys and girls at school. For example, CCHS 136 below draws attention to the norms of appearance and bodily comportment which appear to drive the bitching amongst girls, while boys, who are also capable of such behaviour, are constructed as dealing with it in more physically aggressive ways. Her comment that boys tend to provoke 'bitch fights' amongst girls, while the latter ignore boys' physical fights, suggests that boys derive a sense of pleasure and power from inciting girls to engage in such practices but the reverse is not held to be true. Furthermore, she sees the whole issue of bullying as an inevitable part of school life and as the only way to solve the problems that arise. This resonates with many students' assertions that bullying or teasing was a 'normal' or an expected part of school life:

- School for me, being a girl, is difficult concerning bitchiness and fitting in. People have set groups and only a few people are able to come out of these groups and have friends with everyone. I'm not especially a popular or loser, as we call them at school. These names are used at school, it sort of puts people down and they lose their self-esteem ... Girls generally are very bitchy, they have set standards of what and how we should act and dress. Thus for some people it is hard as we all aren't as fortunate as others. Boys also at this school are just as bitchy as the girls but seem to handle it in different ways. They act physically, whereas girls just bitch and call names ... When boys see girls having a bitch fight they find it pathetic but they also try to provoke it. But when boys have fights, girls see it as pathetic, and don't see the point of it. In conclusion, I believe that most people probably see school life in the same way as I, as a whole lot of problems that can only be solved by fighting (CCHS F 136/16).

GHS 29 also draws attention to the gendered regimes of harassment regarding the different role that the deployment of sexuality plays in boys' and girls' lives. In short, boys use sexuality to call into question and to police both girls' and boys' reputations, with the former subjected to the risk of being labelled a 'slut' or a lesbian and the latter a 'fag'.

- Being a girl in school I think would be more tough than boys. Girls are extremely bitchy. When girls are not bitching they are usually thinking about it ... Because girls are bitchy, they form little groups. For instance in my school there are the upper class snobs, middle class snobs, lower class snobs. There are people who don't want, won't or can't be in these little groups so they form one of their own. Also being a girl, if you are good friends with a guy you have automatically created a rumour about yourself. Rumours that are most common for girls are: pregnancy, lesbian or bi-sexual, slut. And because girls are bitchy they thrive on gossip thus leading to a rumour. With boys I think that the issues that they are faced with mainly consist

of sex (or therefore lacking of). That is what girls are
fed anyway through teenybopper girl magazines.
Perhaps there is also the factor of questioning sexuality and fighting (GHS F 29/15).

However, there was a tendency for some students to assert that boys were more honest or direct in how they dealt with conflict and this was constructed as a positive gendered attribute set against girls' devalued bitching behaviours:

- The good thing about guys is that they are honest. If they don't like someone, they're mean and rude or there's violence. I actually prefer this to the constant gossip and 'bitching' that goes on with the girls. Girls no matter where you go or who you are, they bitch. Bitching sessions are a major problem with the girls. These little fights are usually over guys (CCHS F 14/16).

- Boys at school will usually argue then fight each other (fists). Girls on the other hand bitch each other and usually one of the girls gets teased so much that they leave. After boys have a fight, within a few days or weeks, they are the best of friends. Girls don't do it that way. I believe it is a lot easier for boys to go to school and enjoy it than girls coming to school (GHS M 218/15).

The above boy indicates that dealing overtly with conflict in the way boys do means that the tension is resolved, while this is not the case with girls bitching, which he suggests persists over long periods of time with the latter never really resolving the underlying tensions. For this reason, he asserts that life is much easier for boys than for girls at school. Similarly, the following boy is peeved by girls' bitching behaviour, which he considers to be motivated by trivial matters that are not worth the attention they receive:

- A good thing about being a guy is that guys don't really bitch between each other whereas girls just don't stop. At school, nearly every day, some girls will

> be fighting over some things as little as 'you went to someone else's house instead of mine' to things like 'you kissed my boyfriend, you slut!' This gets really annoying because it is so pathetic especially when they talk about each other behind their backs (GHS M 267/16).

However, other boys raise questions about the role of fighting as a means of gaining respect from their peers, as well as asserting masculine power. In this sense, fighting is a social practice through which boys are able or required to prove their masculinity on particular occasions at school (see Canaan, 1991; Salisbury & Jackson, 1996). Swain writes about how boys are concerned about the maintenance and appearance of their bodies, learning to 'control' their bodies, 'acquiring and mastering a number of techniques' and using them in the appropriate ways that being a boy demands (2003: 300). Utilising Bourdieu's notion of 'embodied' capital, Swain argues that the body can be seen as possessing a 'physical capital': 'bodies may have power, status and/or an array of distinctive symbolic forms that the boys are able to draw on and use as resources that bring agency and influence' (2003: 301). The body becomes the

> main resource to construct their masculinity and gain and establish peer group status ... the body is used to act tough and hard, and as a socio-cultural symbol ... the body forms a major constituent of dominant and subordinated forms of masculinity (2003: 311).

Thus, while for girls 'physical capital' is about having a body for display and ornamentation, being able to physically fight with the body becomes a signifier of a dominant masculinity. Renold's research showed how 'more gentle and non-sporting boys' were more often positioned as 'heterosexual failures' and subject to harassment and ridicule, particularly if their subordinated masculinity meant they were relating to 'non-desirable' girls or relating to girls in general in ways that were emotional rather than overtly physically sexual:

> usually for pursuing or being pursued by 'non-desirable' girls ... For the majority of girls ... the most sought after boys constituted the 'A' team (football) ... physical or emotional closeness to girls could be both masculinity confirming and masculinity denying (2003: 182).

This regime of the policing of masculinity (Martino, 2000) is reflected in the following boys' comments:

- School is like you have to stick up for yourself sometimes and get respect, so you don't get pushed around all the time ... Being a boy at school means you have to be careful about what you say to people or you might get beaten up (GHS M 201/14).

- I think it's good being a boy, because we look a bit more powerful than the girls and we don't take shit (GHS M 202/15).

- I think boys at school have to maintain their 'macho' image in front of all the other boys, sometimes this can lead to bullying and fighting and people getting picked on etc. But most of the times it's just because a lot of people have nothing better to do than to bully other people. I think it is sometimes worse for boys than for girls in the day to day like at school ... (GSH M 223/15).

The association of fighting with fashioning a particular version of masculinity is made explicit when GHS 223 mentions that boys have to 'maintain their macho image' and when GHS 202 actually constructs boys as more powerful in comparison to girls because they 'don't take shit' (see also Mills, 2001).

While many students tended to value boys' honesty in terms of how they dealt with interpersonal conflict, the following boy asserted that they still 'bullshit more':

- Being a boy at school is alright. You get into more fights, you don't go around bitching about everyone but you probably bullshit more (GHS M 256/14).

Thus, while boys may not 'go around bitching' about one another, this boy suggests – through his use of the word 'bullshit' – that boys still try to impress one another through what might be identified as a form of macho bravado which is as equally dishonest as the practice of bitching. This underside of macho posturing is targeted for criticism by another boy at this government high school where there tended to be a definite culture of fighting amongst the boys:

- At school I have to deal with bitchiness from girls and boys. Girls at an age of teenager bitch on so much that you can't stand it, they go around saying they love this person and then they go and root somebody else behind your back. Boys go around saying that they are macho but when it comes down to it backfires and they shit their pants. For example they say 'if they do this or don't do that I'll smack the fuck out of them', but when they don't they just let it go like it was nothing. But being a boy has got its advantages because things just blow over and they can be better the next day. Also you can go get pissed and have a jam so I call it and say na I was just pissed I'm sorry, but don't say you didn't enjoy it. I believe that just girls have to deal with physical problems such as their monthly activities, I'm sure you know what I mean (bloody). But boys have problems of being accepted into a group. I'm in the biggest group in Year 10. We go around making X school worth its name. But all this is for nothing. If you don't turn in a heart beat, one day they love ya the next they diss ya [reject or criticise you], it's all shit (GHS M 271/15).

The contradictions here are noteworthy in terms of how this boy inscribes masculinity. On one level he rejects the way boys make empty threats to assert their masculinity, but when actually confronted do not act. But, on another level, he likes how boys deal with conflict – apparently, once it is addressed it 'blow[s] over'. The other privilege he cites is that boys 'getting pissed' and having sex are then able to use alcohol as an excuse. He appears to diminish social problems girls face by claiming that *just* girls have to deal with physical problems' (our emphasis), which he contrasts with the social problems of boys having to gain acceptance into a peer group. However, by the time we reach the end of the 'script', we are told that he is part of the biggest group at school and that they have a reputation. But his next statement reveals how precarious such power is and how it can be lost in a 'heart beat'. This boy's response draws attention to the precarious nature of dominant 'cool' masculinity and how easily it can be threatened. In fact, one gets the sense that he lives in constant fear of losing his power within his peer group, which apparently can be taken away so easily.

BEING A GIRL IS BETTER THAN BEING A BOY

For these reasons, a number of girls claimed that they would much rather be a girl than a boy at school:

- I would much rather be a girl at school than a boy. This is because I think girls create more of a tighter circle of friends so they have lots of support. I think that boys would have to deal with a few more issues than girls. Boys are meant to be all macho and tough and not show their feelings. For, e.g., it is not uncommon for a girl to be crying or upset at school, however if a boy cried then he would get teased etc. I think that most issues are common to both boys and girls, however on a different level of importance. Girls tend to be bitchy and make a big issue about friends and 'who's not talking to who' but guys don't really fuss about issues like that. They're more concerned about maintaining their 'tough, bad boy' image (GHS F 46/15).

- It is pretty good being a girl, I would hate to be a boy. Most boys get into fights (GHS F 55/15).

One boy from the rural government high school, who was subjected to harassment, abuse and bullying also claimed that he would prefer to be a girl:

- Personally, I would rather want to be a girl because girls are nicer ... and communicate better ... but I know there are some bitches out there who harass other girls too ... boys usually get assaulted and bullied by other boys and girls usually have to deal with boys' stupid behaviour. I think if I was a girl I would be happier at school and if I was a lesbian I wouldn't have to deal with boys (RGHS M 1/15).

His reference to lesbians not having to deal with boys is based on the assumption that they would no longer be the object of boys' attention and, hence, harassing behaviours due to their sexual orientation.

IMMATURE BOYS

The discourse of 'immaturity' to justify boys' harassment, particularly boys' bullying, as discussed in previous chapters, constructs an essentialised linear psychological development of social behaviour that was often taken up by girls to explain boys' behaviour, and thereby reiterates normative backlash debates that can justify and verify bullying as innate or part of the 'normal' development of young people. For example, CCHS 97 below sees 'immaturity' as driving the Year 8 boys' antisocial behaviours in the locker areas at her school:

- The problem with school is that some people mature faster than others. Some people are still acting like kids in high school and they cop a lot from it. Year 8s are very different from Year 12s at school. The locker areas are separated into year groups. I recently walked through the Year 8 area before school and was really pelleted with food stolen from people's bags and narrowly missed a herd of 3 feet pimply boys slamming each other into lockers. Luckily they saw me and they retreated shamefully into a quiet conversation about computer games. It was almost as if I were a superior race. The school split into upper and lower levels, but Year 8s are still put into the same category as Year 10s, but that can't really be changed. At least we can look forward to peace in Year 11 (CCHS F 97/14).

In her research, Francis found that 'femininity was constructed as sensible and selfless, and masculinity as silly and selfish' (2000: 52) and there are definitely traces of such a discourse in several girls' responses in terms of how they account for boys' behaviours (see also Hey et al., 2001):

- There are a couple of guys that still haven't matured and still like to tease people and it's quite annoying (GHSV F 81/16).

Moreover, Francis adds that students 'in their discussions of gendered classroom behaviour ... reconceptualised the sensible/silly dichotomy in terms of maturity and immaturity' (2000: 50). However, discourses about differing maturity levels for boys and girls can often be used as a means by which to trivialise and legitimate boys' harassing, antisocial behaviours as just another instance of boys being boys. Furthermore, it can also be deployed to downplay the social responsibility that boys themselves need to take for their own behaviour (see Martino & Beckett, 2004). For example, this discourse of immaturity is used to explain and account for boys' tendency to resort to fighting at school as opposed to actually 'talking out' the problem:

- The sort of issues boys have to deal with aren't the same. I found out that most fights are between guys because they never talk it out. I find them immature ... Showing themselves as big men or tough guys I feel is plain stupid. Why aren't we all equal. There always has to be someone who's better. These are most ideas of what boys deal with (GHS F 122/15).

However, what is interesting about this response is that the immaturity of the boys is not seen as a natural consequence of their biology. Rather it is linked, for this girl, to the need boys feel to display themselves as appropriately masculine and, hence, as 'tough guys'. The issue of biology was also raised in relation to bitching, where some girls saw it as an innate quality of being a girl, and yet, as SSGS 146 discusses below, the links to social cultures and hierarchies are usually presented simultaneously:

- Girls are born bitches ... It's so frustrating how girls

can't be honest with each other just in case it wasn't seen as being 'cool' (SSGS 146/16).

THE CONSEQUENCES OF BULLYING

Overall, the survey responses highlight the significant impact of bullying on the lives of boys and girls at school and draw attention to the need for schools to address and understand its gendered dimensions (Duncan, 1999; Alloway, 2000). As RGHS 28 indicates earlier in this chapter, the 'bitchiness' was so severe that her grades began to suffer. Other researchers have indicated that severe forms of harassment at school can have damaging emotional and psychological consequences for young people, even leading some to consider suicide (see Laskey & Beavis, 1996; Goldflam et al., 1999; Mills, 2001; Dorais, 2004), particularly if young people feel helpless in dealing with it, or feel unsupported by the school:

- It's like a silent war, which group knows better guys, which group goes to more parties etc. It can be really stressful sometimes. Eventually the competition turns into hostility ... You just feel shit cos you never wanted anyone to hate you, in fact the complete opposite (SSGS 119/15).

- I am not attracted to females and therefore recess and lunch breaks mean that me and my friends sit down and talk about all those handsome boys we met on the weekend (sometimes very draining) ... Sometimes problems between friends occur usually purely out of jealousy. The problems can be frustrating and can often drive one out of concentrating on school and work (SSGS 6/15).

- Bullying are issues that still happen ... I have been a victim and no-one including teachers can do anything about it because they're always 'busy' with issues themselves ... more care should be taken toward the students! (GHSV F 194/16).

- If everyone's friends are nice and in a good mood, it's usually a fun day, however if they are mean and teasing me about everything, then it is bad ... sometimes I get bagged and teased a lot about appearance etc because people think I'm a bit of a clown and that I don't mind, but it does hurt me a lot (SSGS 16/15).

Goldflam, Chadwick & Brown for example draw links between sexuality and suicide, claiming that 'young people with same sex attraction [are] at high risk of isolation, marginalisation, depression and self-harm' (1999: 9; see also Kendall, 1998; Pallotta-Chiarolli, 2005b). Moreover, they draw attention to how susceptible these young people are to harassment and how it impacts on their mental health. In fact, research in the United States has found that those students who either identify as or are suspected to be gay, lesbian, bisexual or transgender are at risk of being harassed at school by both their peers and teachers and that these behaviours can impact detrimentally on their learning, leading them to drop out of school (see Uribe & Harbeck, 1992; Goldflam et al., 1999). This is supported by evidence we have presented in previous chapters regarding boys' narratives about the prevalence of homophobic harassment at school and also by girls who talked about boys labelling them as lesbians for failing to meet up to their expectations of acceptable femininity. What needs to be emphasised is that the harassment is often an effect of 'category maintenance work' designed to police acceptable versions of masculinity and femininity at school through regimes of compulsory heterosexuality.

- I find that boys are only a problem to me because society and friends make it one. I am still unaware of my sexual preference but if I am bisexual or lesbian the only reason why I would hide it (if I hide it) will most likely be because of my friends as they are fairly narrow minded in that area which upsets me (SSGS 126/16).

RACIAL DIMENSIONS OF BULLYING

Racial discrimination or discrimination on the basis of ethnicity was also mentioned by both girls and boys as a problem impacting on their lives at school (4% of entire cohort). A Chilean girl mentioned how her darker skin had led her to be targeted for racist abuse on the basis that it was a signifier of Aboriginality:

- At school you may be treated different because you are weaker or because you look different. When I was in primary school I used to be bullied by older kids because I was darker than them. I was called ABC Aboriginal Bum Cleaner but I am not Aboriginal (RGHS F 22/14/Chilean).

A Fijian-Scottish girl also recounts a horrific story of racial and physical abuse when she first started school:

- Around 10 years ago I started school. Everything up till then was good. I don't have good memories of starting off. All I can remember was me, a scared little girl who thought school was like a prison and I was uncomfortable. In Year 1 I had problems with a boy who was in Year 6. He used to hit me and smack my head against bins because of my racial background because I have a black mother. This was about the time I didn't trust anyone. I wondered why kids could be so cruel. Why they looked at skin colour and they couldn't look beyond it (RGHS F 27/16/Fijian-Scottish).

Students from Asian backgrounds also mentioned racist behaviour directed toward them at school:

- Racial problems are the most which influence me ... This school has many problems ... specially Asians tend to face the most problems. Many in this school are RACIST against Asians (CCHS M 33/17/Japanese).

- Well problems that I experience at school are all racial, some people seem to dislike Asians I mean. I got bullied because I have yellow skin and black hair I mean what's the difference. We are all humans but I haven't done anything to offend them, I get called 'chink' and 'gook' and people say 'go back to where you came from', this shit sucks!! If I had the choice I would go back. I don't want to take over anyone's land. Why don't they leave us alone and let us be happy. We work just as hard as everybody else. Please why is it so racist? (CCHS F 106/16/Asian).

The following students also illustrate the extent to which sociocultural factors such as ethnicity and multi-directional racism may also be implicated in bullying and bitching (see also Pallotta-Chiarolli, 2000; Martino & Pallotta-Chiarolli, 2003):

- There are some really bitch skips [Anglo-Australians] that are racist and you really need to teach them how to respect you (GHSV F 79/16/Chinese).

- I have to put up with racism cos I'm black (GHSV M 89/16/Sri Lankan).

- Some friends are really cruel when for example a new Indian girl comes and they say 'Why didn't you tell me she is black?' It's the same with the Asian population, they all seem to be in one certain group and I often hear girls complaining about having so many Asians in the school and how they can't talk properly (SSGS 44/15).

In fact, for students from culturally diverse backgrounds the issue of whiteness (Aveling, 1998; Martino, 2003) emerged as a significant influence driving the normalisation that they encountered from other students at school:

- For someone coming from an Asian background studying here in Australia is very troublesome. It began in Year 9. Black hair, small eyes and yellow skin is a description which is not difficult to miss and although it was only verbal abuse it has caused me to

view the Australian society in a very different manner.
I have learnt that how you look, how you talk and how
you act reflects greatly which society you belong to.
Such discrimination coming from my fellow students ...
Although I am certainly not implying that all
Australians are prejudiced, in fact, [during] my stay
here I have met many decent and respectful
Australians who are very down to earth. My message is
that it has greatly affected my studies here in
Australia.
   PS. What the fuck do the racists think they are!!
We Asians have nothing against them, we have done
nothing to hurt or harm them! (CCHS F 10816/Chinese).

- People pick on you and are racist and sexist and think
you're crap ... I am not Aboriginal, but my sister is and
she gets enough shit from everyone, including my step-
dad, she doesn't need it any more. People need to grow
up and respect each other a little more (GHS F 70/15).

The following boy, who identifies himself as 'a white Australian', is also subjected to harassment because he chooses to befriend others from culturally diverse backgrounds:

- I often see racist people at school who offend me
and other people. Although I am a white Australian, I am
friends with people from all over the world e.g UK, Italy,
Spain, Japan, SE Asia, America etc. I sometimes get shit
because of it, but there is nothing I can do about it and
I don't really care because despite threats I ignore
them wholeheartedly and no malice has ever been
directed against me. Bullies are everywhere at my
school, but I have learned to accept it and they don't
scare me ... I have had threats but nothing has ever
materialised. But some people live in fear. I find that
disgusting that some people are too busy putting others
down and some people are believing them (CCHS M 4/15).

Thus a racist white mentality is also identified as driving bullying practices at school, with this boy indicating that some students live in fear of being targeted because of their cultural background. In fact, this is supported by the following girls who claim that being a 'normal Australian', which means being white, is a significant factor contributing to their avoidance of discrimination at school:

- School is good for me because I hardly have any problems. Apart from the work, I often enjoy it because I can see my friends and socialise. I think since I have an Australian background, I'm not singled out as much as some for being different to others (CCHS F 161/15).

- For me, school is a very enjoyable place. I enjoy coming to it and I have no real problems with getting along with people or being discriminated against. But maybe that's just me, maybe I'm a lucky one who doesn't have to worry about those sort of things because I'm a normal Australian girl who is of above average intelligence, good at sport, therefore, no-one really hassles me about anything and I have no real problems/issues. But I do realise that many other girls and boys face serious problems each time they enter the school grounds. Many are classified into the intelligent and not so intelligent groups, then into whether you're cool or uncool, then whether you are Australian or of other background (although in this school it's not of great importance, especially for me because I have a number of Asian friends). After being classified by these titles, each student belongs to a group and they find comfort in people who are of the same background/ intelligence etc as themselves (CCHS F 142/16).

Both these girls are able to escape the forms of harassment documented by many other students in this chapter because they fit into the normalised category of being a privileged white Anglo-Australian. CCHS 142, however, situates this issue of normality within broader frameworks of classification involving the requirement to act 'cool', which ties in with maintaining a particular image or reputation. As many other students have documented in this chapter, managing this practice of 'fitting in' is a difficult and risky business with the constant threat of harassment and ostracism an important consideration in negotiating social relationships at school.

CONCLUSION

This chapter has highlighted the very significant ways in which bullying and harassment in schools are gendered in quite specific ways, with the threat of physical violence emerging as a significant reality for boys in their social relationships with one another at school. For girls, however, the impact and effects of bitchiness surfaced as particularly significant and equally destructive to their emotional and psychological well-being. It is therefore important to understand and to emphasise that non-physical forms of bullying, such as verbal taunting and intimidatory looks, impact in equally detrimental ways on both boys and girls at school (see Goldflam et al., 1999; Lipkin, 1999; Plummer, 1999; Tanenbaum, 2002; Dorais, 2004).

GENDER-BASED HARASSMENT IN SCHOOLS

AIM • To develop a deep understanding about the gendered dimensions of bullying in schools

GENDERED DIMENSIONS OF BULLYING FOR GIRLS

'Bitchiness' is one of the major forms of harassment and exclusion practised by girls against their same-sex peers.

'Bitchiness' is linked to 'coolness', popularity and competition amongst girls.

Not all girls subscribe to this form of harassment. It is not a natural consequence of being a girl.

GENDERED DIMENSIONS OF BULLYING FOR BOYS

Boys are often presented as engaging in more physical forms of bullying directed at their same-sex peers.

Fighting is seen by some boys as a means by which to prove their masculinity.

Boys' harassment is often trivialised or explained in terms of their immaturity.

A WHOLE SCHOOL APPROACH TO ADDRESSING BULLYING

Addressing bullying initially means understanding that it is not a natural consequence of some Darwinian notion of survival of the fittest.

Bullying is often about enforced normalisation and involves policing acceptable versions of masculinity and femininity in schools. It can also have racial dimensions.

DISCUSSION FORUM

THEME 1 • **BOYS FIGHT AND GIRLS BITCH**

From your reading of the students' comments below, how would you account for or explain the differences between the boys' and girls' approaches to bullying? How might such gender issues be addressed in schools?

> • Boys get in fights and get called gay but girls get in bitch fights all the time and heaps of gossip goes around every day and girls get reputations as sluts, bitches that can stay with them until they leave school. A problem with boys sometimes is in the change rooms at sport time but girls aren't really the same, they don't really make fun of each other or anything. Boys get in physical fights, but bitching can lower people's self esteem and confidence. There are so many labels in school, 'bitch', 'slut', 'gay', 'squid', 'try hard', 'freak'. A lot of these things change once you leave school. You can get called desperate if you go out with someone younger or in a younger level if you aren't in school as you are thought of as an age not a grade, you aren't judged as much (CCHS F 97/14).

> • Girls are actually harsher than guys although it is only verbal. Guys get physical (GHSV F 116/16).

> • Girls have to deal with bitchiness and body image. Boys have to deal with bullying and competitiveness and body image (SSGS 56/15).

> • Sometimes I just get sick of the amount of bitching and back-stabbing that can happen but boys don't have all those complications (SSGS 77/15).

> • I think girls are just as bitchy as boys and boys gossip just as much as girls if not more (SSGS 107/16).

160   Being normal is the only way to be

THEME 2 • **THE IMPACT OF BITCHINESS ON GIRLS' LIVES**

What are the different forms of 'bitchiness' that the following girls draw attention to? What exactly do the following girls say about the impact of 'bitchiness' on their lives? How might this be dealt with in schools?

- Being a girl you sometimes feel pressured by your peers to compete materialistically such as wearing make-up, jewellery, losing weight, dying your hair etc. Also some girls can be quite bitchy involving boys and materialism (GHSV F 182/16).

- Being a girl at school you always feel you can't be yourself because you will be ignored and not heard if you are different from others by how you look ... seems like people say anything that even they don't know that it really hurts inside you and if it goes too far words can kill someone ... I face a lot of problems towards my weight, I don't get abused by it but I seem to feel this by their sound of voice and their expression (GHSV F 180/16).

- I usually tell people if they've got a massive pimple or they stink etc, which is probably mean but it's happened whilst I've been here and I like that bluntness (SSGS 62/15).

- As girls we are very bitchy and try our hardest to make certain girls miserable ... (SSGS 64/15).

- Being at a more expensive school and surrounded by rich people can get a bit annoying because families such as mine are in the working and comfortable class of society and some people at school will act a bit spoilt and make people like me feel less worthy, however, it doesn't really bother me because you can choose not to associate with them and because I have a group of friends who are mainly of European/Arabic background (SSGS 2/15/Italian).

- There are set groups and you either belong to that one and no-one else's like there are many cliques and you can't really 'mingle' with the other ones ... girls have to deal with lots of things pertaining to social drama ... I just think girls are drama queens (SSGS 118/16).

- It's really bad cos sometimes I see my friends bullying other girls in our group. It's hard to know what to do in these kinds of situations. Girls will often put down others because they are envious and jealous and this makes them lose confidence because the jealous girls tease them (SSGS 105/16).

- There is so much bitchiness and people are not caring about other people's feelings. This bothers me because when I arrive at school no matter how happy I am, I am reminded of this and I feel upset and horrible and then I find it hard to focus in class (SSGS 149/16).

7

DEVELOPING STUDENT WELFARE POLICIES: A whole school approach to gender and social justice

IN THIS CHAPTER YOU WILL:

- synthesise the reading of previous chapters to build a threshold knowledge about gender and sexuality;
- apply a teacher threshold knowledge about gender and schooling to school-based welfare policies, and position this within a framework of a social justice.

INTRODUCTION

Each of the previous chapters has used student voice to build a specific knowledge about what it means to be 'normal' for young people in schools and how this impacts on their lives. The workshop activities at the end of each chapter are designed and included to function as professional development forums for teachers in schools. These provide a platform for teachers to explore issues of power, gender, sexuality and difference in terms of how they impact on boys' and girls' lives at school, and to consider the implications for their own school context. The series of workshops or forums are also designed to feed into developing school-based welfare policies committed to creating more effective school cultures that celebrate diversity and encourage student participation in the school's management and decision-making processes.

As Alloway argues: 'In an unfortunate slide from well articulated educational principles and values, the voices of students themselves suggest that the political rhetoric has not translated into everyday reality for many girls and boys, particularly with reference to levels of sex-based harassment enacted and experienced at school' (2000: 7–8). There is often a tendency to deny the blatantly gendered and sexualised nature of harassment in schools, which is erased through adopting the umbrella term of bullying to encompass all behaviours that are designed to diminish 'another person simply because of the way they identify as male or female' (2000: 10). As we have repeatedly pointed out, absent from many student welfare policies in schools is a politicised focus on bullying. This absence is supported by a culture that trivialises or ignores the sexist, gendered and homophobic dimensions of harassment among students. Thus, the main objective of the Professional Development forums at the end of each of the previous chapters in this book has been to foreground the politicised dimensions of social relations for young people in schools, particularly with regards to what it means to be 'cool', which is often equated with being a 'normal' guy or girl, i.e. performing your masculinity or femininity in culturally acceptable ways.

This chapter will now outline a framework for developing a whole school approach to gender and social justice that embraces an ethic of pastoral care, one which pays attention to the impact of hierarchical power relationships on young people's lives at school. This brings us to the first step in (re)formulating a school-based welfare policy that is committed to gender justice for girls and boys.

1. BUILDING A THRESHOLD KNOWLEDGE ABOUT GENDER AND SEXUAL POLITICS

The workshop activities at the end of each chapter are designed to build this knowledge by using student voice. This knowledge can be built further in the local context by undertaking a similar audit of student experiences at your school through administering an anonymous questionnaire. This would include asking students to respond to questions such as the following:

- What is school like for you?
- Can you write about any problems that you are experiencing at school?
- What are the positive things about school?
- Are there issues that just girls or just boys have to deal with at school? Can you write about these?
- How would you improve school to make it a safer and/or better environment for learning?

Doing such an audit after engaging in the workshop activities in this book provides a useful foundation upon which to start articulating a pastoral care and student welfare policy which names sexuality and the gendered body as central to developing a deep understanding about the policing of masculinity and femininity in schools that can result in particular forms of bullying. It also raises broader issues of how 'being really cool' or 'being normal', which entails being a particular sort of girl or boy, can have particular ramifications for students and teachers in schools in terms of feeling safe and feeling motivated to learn.

A final step is to structure staff meetings, discussions and professional development forums around the responses from anonymous students in your school. This is a very powerful method of addressing the realities within schools in a way that they cannot be denied or undermined. This strategy is particularly useful in working with teacher resistance or trivialisation of any issues. It may be easy to dismiss a colleague's concerns about gendered injustices and homophobia, but it is far more difficult to ignore the documented experiences, insights and concerns of students in our schools.

2. REVIEWING EXISTING SCHOOL-BASED WELFARE POLICIES THROUGH ADOPTING A PARTICULAR LENS OR SOCIAL JUSTICE FRAMEWORK THAT SIGNALS A COMMITMENT TO NAMING CERTAIN FORMS OF POWER

The following questions are designed to facilitate this process and can be used in conjunction with the results from the student audit as outlined above:

- Is homophobia named and addressed as a particular form of harassment?
- Are terms such as 'compulsory heterosexuality', 'heterosexism' and 'sexuality' used within the context of creating safe school cultures and environments free of all forms of harassment at school?
- Are masculinity and femininity specifically mentioned in relation to understanding what it means to be 'cool' and how this knowledge is useful in acquiring a deep understanding of social acceptance and peer group dynamics for girls and boys in schools?
- How might articulating a specific focus on the policing of masculinity and femininity in the policy add to a deeper understanding of gender and sexual politics in the lives of boys and girls at school?
- Is the word 'power' specifically mentioned?
- How might the following questions help to focus the policy reformulation more specifically on power issues in students' lives?
    - What does it mean to be 'normal' or 'cool'?
    - Who decides this?
    - What are the consequences for those who fail to measure up to what is considered to be 'normal' or 'cool'?
- To what extent is there a commitment to valuing student input and voice through including them in the school's decision-making processes?

3. INCORPORATING THRESHOLD KNOWLEDGE ABOUT GENDER AND SOCIAL JUSTICE INTO THE EXISTING CURRICULUM

This involves explicitly articulating a commitment to productive pedagogies or quality teaching and learning in schools. A whole school approach needs to avoid simply adding on a focus on gender and diversity to the health education curriculum. It involves articulating at the school-based policy level a commitment to addressing the four dimensions of productive learning and teaching in schools throughout the curriculum:

- a high degree of intellectual quality: To what extent is there a focus on higher order and problem solving tasks for students? To what extent are deficit models of the student being actively disregarded?
- high levels of connectedness in terms of curriculum content and its application to the students' lives outside of school: To what extent is the curriculum across all subject areas committed to making connections with the real worlds and lives of students outside of school?
- supportive classroom environments where students feel valued and are encouraged to take risks in their learning: To what extent are students actively involved in formulating ground rules for respectful interaction and positive learning?
- a strong recognition and celebration of difference: To what extent is there an active attempt to avoid stereotyping students on the basis of their ethnicity, race, sexuality, social class background and gender? (see Lingard , B, Martino, W, Mills, M & Bahr, M, 2003).

Each of these four dimensions involves an avoidance of a simplistic 'tips for teachers' approach to addressing the educational and social needs of boys and girls in schools while acknowledging the need for a very specific knowledge base about the gendered dimensions of what it means to be normal. In other words, the social construction of gender, what it means to be male or female, needs to be understood in schools. As international research consistently shows, how certain versions of masculinity and femininity are defined and validated in our culture does have an impact on the self-concept, attitudes and behaviours of young people in terms of what is considered desirable or 'cool'. In viewing such behaviours as fixed or biologically determined attributes, what is emphasised is the inevitability of such forms of power and a certain denial of learned dimensions and the ideological significance of social attitudes.

In this sense, addressing each of the above dimensions must be understood within the context of providing for student welfare in terms of creating safe school environments for students to learn and to achieve their potential. This is an integral part of creating what Ancess (2003) terms 'a community of caring'. This involves a consideration and clear articulation of a sound philosophical basis for establishing an agreed upon understanding of the purposes of schooling and the role of the student in the provision of civics education. The following questions, particularly if raised in relation to the findings from the student audit, need to be debated, discussed and used to inform current school-based welfare policies:

- What is the purpose of schooling?
- What does it mean to be an active and responsible citizen and what contribution should the school make to producing such a citizen?
- To what extent should students be encouraged to challenge authority and power in schools?
- What sorts of values and priorities are considered important?
- How is the dignity and respect of each individual student to be maintained?
- How is difference and diversity understood and addressed from a social justice and gender justice standpoint?

TEMPLATE FOR FORMULATING SCHOOL-BASED WELFARE POLICIES

STAGE 1 • **BUILDING A TEACHER THRESHOLD KNOWLEDGE ABOUT GENDER AND DIVERSITY**

What knowledge about gender and sexuality is useful in addressing student welfare and well-being issues? (see chapters 3 and 4)

OTHER QUESTIONS

- What is the relationship between being 'macho' and being 'cool'?
- What is meant by the term, 'policing masculinity'?
- Why is it useful to think about masculinity and femininity in the plural?
- What do we learn from the students about what it means to be a normal boy?
- Is homophobia just something that affects gay or non-heterosexual students?
- How is femininity policed for girls?
- How do boys influence the way girls see or perceive themselves?
- What is considered to be normal femininity for girls?
- To what extent do appearance and body image impact on girls' social relationships?
- What is meant by the term 'different classes of girls'?

STAGE 2 • **REFORMULATING SCHOOL-BASED WELFARE POLICIES**

What understandings about sex-based harassment, homophobia, heterosexism and compulsory heterosexuality need to inform the recasting or revision of current school-based policies? (see chapters 5 and 6)

OTHER QUESTIONS

- In what ways do boys harass girls?
- How is boys' harassment of girls related to asserting masculine superiority?
- Why is it that the most heavily teased girls are those who do not conform to some boys' construction of normal or desirable femininity?
- Are there different forms of bullying that are gendered?
- What are the similarities and differences between the bullying behaviours of boys and girls?
- How is immaturity used to dismiss the severity and degree of boys' harassing or problematic behaviour?
- What are the consequences of bullying?
- What other forms of bullying can be identified?

STAGE 3 • INCORPORATING A FOCUS ON PEDAGOGICAL REFORM

What social structures and systems of power/authority impede productive teacher/student relationships? (see chapters 1 and 2)

OTHER QUESTIONS

- What criticisms do boys and girls make about schooling and approaches to discipline/behaviour management?
- What kinds of school structures and relationships with students lead them to develop more autonomy and to take more responsibility for their own learning?
- What contributes to or exacerbates resistance to authoritarian uses of power or discipline in schools?
- Do single-sex classes per se provide better educational and social outcomes for students?
- How might school culture, structures and/or approaches to teaching reinforce dominant masculinity or passive femininity?
- What is the problem with the rationale behind separating boys from girls or vice versa in order to avoid being distracted by the opposite sex?

- What forms of resistance to school-based authority and teachers do girls demonstrate?
- How does menstruation impact on girls' experiences of schooling?
- To what extent are school subjects and ideas about success gendered?
- How does 'fitting in' and being normal impact on students' learning at school?

8

CONCLUSION:
Questioning what it means to be 'really cool'

Our research found that being 'really cool' entails embracing a particular sort or version of what it means to be a 'normal' boy or a 'normal' girl. However, there were many students who struggled with such normalisation and actively questioned these power relationships. In this book our aim has been to present the views and opinions of these students. While many teachers have indicated they 'know' about the experiences of students at school, our intention has been to provide educators with raw data in the form of students writing about their lives at school. We have also outlined ways of using these voices in Professional Development forums and workshops for teachers and illustrated how these voices might be used as a basis for stimulating discussion about a range of issues impacting on students' lives at school. We see in such critical questioning and thinking a productive potential for feeding into a recasting of school-based welfare and gender equity policies that address issues such as:

- creating a safe school environment;
- developing a democratic school culture where students' opinions and perspectives are valued;
- addressing the sex- and gender-based dimensions of bullying;
- addressing issues of diversity in schools;
- working with the links between peer group hierarchies and learning.

In reading the student narratives and writing this book, we have had a sense of revisiting what has already been said, what has already been raised, and what continues to be erased in backlash educational policy and debate (Lingard & Douglas, 1999). As Weaver-Hightower states: 'Many studies conclude with the rather standard, though important, finding that the gender regimes of schools ... make for a "chilly climate" or "reinforce the larger gender order" in society' (2003: 488). However, we have wanted to signal an awareness in our research of the shifts in the masculinities and femininities available to young people. As Lesko explores, consumer forces, marketing to children and adolescents, technological developments whereby young people have direct access to a whole 'web of information and lives without the traditional adult censor/mediator', and popular culture, have all led to children becoming 'erotic, spectacular, and marketable' (2000: 198). We have seen this in the way 'bully boys' and 'bitch Barbies' construct and perform a gendered, classed and (hetero)sexualised self. The boundary between adolescence and adulthood is 'blurred' and educators need to acknowledge the need to interrogate both 'minoritizing and universalizing discourses of children and teenagers' (2000: 198). A monolithic view of adolescents as supposedly all the same and as fundamentally different to and ignorant in relation to adults can no longer be held. Teenagers need to be

> active participants (not tokens) in educational and other public policy deliberations ... I am not just trumpeting one 'student voice' but calling for the imagining of concrete practices in which youth demand and exercise adultlike responsibilities ... What counts as a public problem and how 'needs' are conceptualised constitute a major part of political life today (2000: 199).

However, as we have argued in this book, young people's lives at school get framed and circumscribed with minimal engagement and consultation with the young people themselves.

We also found that student narratives have the potential to provide teachers and administrators in schools with the opportunity to explore the interwoven social and educational worlds of young people. In fact, they have opened the door for us to take our readers into the worlds of 'bully boys' and 'bitch Barbies' and this has enabled us to foreground the multiple positionings and intertwining practices of masculinity and femininity in the lives of many boys and girls attending a range of different schools. However, we found that there were many students who questioned the normative constructs of being a boy and being a girl at school or who asserted that they enjoyed school. Thus, in this conclusion, we wanted to reiterate the voices of those students who resisted these practices of normalisation, who redefined what it means to be 'really cool'.

We were also conscious of not wanting to leave our readers with a construction of schooling as a pervasive negative experience for all students. For example, some students were active in attempting to carve out a space of healthy balance in their lives, committed to respectful and caring relationships and to empowered learning. As the following students stated:

- I love school because I feel in our year level there is a real community feel. There are no real mean people in our year level like you see in the movies and the media and I think we are supportive of each other ... I'm dreading leaving school and going to uni because I love it so much (SSGS 162/15).

- We are educated very well ... There is also support for students who need it ... To achieve a balance is my main priority – to do well in school but also have a social life, do sport and music (SSGS 26/15).

- The workload can be demanding but I still enjoy the challenges that school brings and the interesting things that happen in day to day life (SSBS M 4/16).

However, it is important to note that for these students, who accounted for only a small percentage in most schools, possessing a particular form of cultural and class capital and social skilling must play a significant part in their capacity to negotiate hierarchical peer group relations and to resist or manage 'being cool' in ways that other students are not able to (see Bourdieu, 1986; Martino, 1999). Or it might be that simply being a particular sort of boy or girl also means that one has the privilege to resist or to just simply act from a very powerful position as a consequence of already embodying a certain version of masculinity and femininity or gendered 'coolness' or 'normality'. As the following boys indicated:

- School isn't too bad because I am part of the crowd (SSBS 29/15).

- Fortunately I have been blessed with reasonable physical and academic abilities and my particular school provides many parents who will support opportunities as well as facilities. From this base I have been able to do many things and to be involved in interschool teams – Swimming, Athletics, Rugby, Waterpolo. But beside playing the sports themselves my most cherished memories will not be succeeding personally but having breakfast with guys after swimming training or going to the 'after parties' ... (SSBS 38/16).

Thus the effect of embodied gendered 'coolness' and 'normality' coupled with certain class capital may work to position certain students to embrace school and learning while also avoiding the trappings of being positioned lower down the social ladder on the basis of how they do their gender (see Gilbert & Gilbert, 1998; Martino, 1999). In fact, there appeared to be a significant number of girls in the single sex girls' school who embraced a culture of learning and achievement and were not subject to harassment. This did not appear to be as evident in other schools. However, it is important to note that this did not ameliorate the pervasive culture of bitchiness built on hierarchical femininities and body fashioning that many of the girls at this school mentioned as still impacting on their lives and relationships with their peers. It is in this sense that those girls and boys who embrace school be acknowledged more fully here, some of whom with much determination, strength and optimism continue to negotiate their places in contradictory and hierarchical systems of gender normalisation (Martino & Pallotta-

Chiarolli, 2003). As the following girl's comment exemplifies, not all students simply subscribed to 'being cool' and, in fact, actively resisted it:

- School for me is like mass conformity in its greatest form. I think this is the time when people try to all fit into a certain stereotype. There are rules people follow, eg, clothes, opinion, hair, school work – this is a main factor ... People like me and my friends like to rebel against this stereotype and live up to being as we're commonly known here as a 'freak'. This angers and confuses the stereos. It's quite amusing really. People like to live in their conformist worlds and we tend to threaten it ... People call you squares because part of the stereotype is to not do any school work and wag regularly ... People at this school have no motivation and want everything done for them. They don't want to work or think for themselves. They spend most of their time intoxicated and direct as much prejudice and bigotry towards the squares as they can. I frequently hear 'freak' yelled at me as I walk down the hall and I feel proud (GHS F 102/15).

Our research tended to highlight what it means to be 'really normal' for many young people and the material effects of this on their lives, which raises the issue of the need for critical questioning in terms of official pedagogical interventions in schools. This is crucial given that:

> The formal pedagogy of schooling [is] about denying questions of difference to their subjects [and hence] there [is] little official encouragement to engage school students in discussions and relations of power (Hey, 1997: 129–30).

In fact, many of the students in our research concluded that schools were definitely in the business of enforcing conformity to institutional norms in terms of regulating and policing their bodies and social behaviour. This was often seen in opposition to actively encouraging students 'to accept responsibility for their behaviour and to take initiatives for change' (Collins et al., 2000: 101).

CREATING SCHOOLS OF 'BALANCED BODS'

Thus, in presenting what may be seen by some as a book of very negative student evaluations of their schooling, we have endeavoured to make transparent the realities of schooling for many young people. However, we would like to conclude with a focus on what those students in schools said worked for them to facilitate their self-development as 'balanced bods' – as young people who did not succumb to the norms of 'acting cool' in order to forfeit a balanced healthy social life and perspective on the importance of schooling.

What do these 'balanced bods' say is 'really cool' as they resist and redefine dominant discourses of 'normal'? What works for them in schools? What insights do they provide into the possibilities for creating an educational system that actually promotes a nurturing, healthy and meaningful learning environment? Two issues need to be raised here: first, although socioeconomic status was seen as divisive and linked to harassment between students in affluent schools, it also provided the school with the economic means with which to provide excellent resources, facilities and opportunities (Wilkinson et al., 2004). Second, although some girls in the single sex school talked about the power of both the 'bitch Barbies' and the 'visibly absent' boys, some of the girls saw this as outweighed by the advantages of not having boys in the school as they felt the environment was friendlier and more conducive to learning, and that girls experienced less debilitating scrutiny and harassment.

Thus, we are left with fundamental questions such as:

1 To what extent are schools equipped with the economic means to provide excellent resources and opportunities for a healthy social and learning culture?
2 How are backlash educational politics and government initiatives failing to address the socioeconomic basis of many of the concerns in Australian schools? (Wilkinson et al., 2004)
3 How do we realistically name and address the impact of misogyny and homophobia in school and its links to learning for both boys and girls?
4 How do we include an acknowledgment of the implication of

gender hierarchies in bullying between boys, between girls, and between boys and girls in both directions, having its basis in hegemonic constructions of masculinity and its power over same-sex and different-sex relationships?

Currently, we believe backlash educational policies, politics and resourcing are deliberately evading the above questions, and erasing the significant ongoing evidence from schools that calls for the above questions to be addressed (House of Representatives Standing Committee, 2002; see also Pallotta-Chiarolli, 1997).

So let's explore what 'balanced bods' say about what works for them in schools, what is 'really cool':

1. The importance of a friendly and emotionally safe environment in the promotion of and engagement with learning; the interconnection and interdependence of a school's social and learning cultures:

    ● School is good. It's lots of fun, and I enjoy learning new things in a friendly environment … School's a great experience, and although I may not admit it out loud, I love it – friends, learning, the works (SSGS 3/15).

    ● The educational levels are extremely high and the friendship groups are very supportive and comforting for me. Being here is a great pleasure because I have the opportunity to work and express myself in subjects and I also have my wonderful friends by my side to help and support me … I can't picture myself in a better environment (SSGS 6/15).

    ● The environment's friendly and safe. I have a great group of friends who support me when I have any problems (GHSV F 19/16).

    ● My school is a fantastic school at which I gain information and work productively. It is a good place to both work and socialise (GHSV M 44/16).

2 The importance of learning and curriculum that is seen as rounded and useful for young people's future lives, not just in terms of vocational skills but life skills as well:

- I think that education is an important part of life and that I have learnt a lot from school. However, I do also think that schools are too much about learning facts and using formulas and not enough about really thinking (SSBS 25/16).

- I see school as a good preparation for the future. It helps us learn social skills, problem solving, to develop lateral thinking, and how to organise our time efficiently (SSGS 3/15).

- A place that I can learn human relations (GHSV M 137/16).

3 The importance of a 'community' feel to a school and to classes, whereby small classes means young people see the school as personal rather than impersonal, relational rather than hierarchical:

- I love coming to this school, the class sizes are small and the year level is small so it makes it easy to get along with people and get to know them better (SSGS 38/15).

- I love school because I feel in our year level there is a real community feel ... I may just feel this way because I have a large group of friends who would be considered 'cool' but I mix with all other groups and try to be nice to everyone so I'm not really affected by gossip or bullying because no-one feels a need to do that (SSGS 162/15).

4 The importance of friendly but firm effective teachers who are 'real' and 'up to date' with their subject knowledge, teaching methods, and understanding of the 'multiple lifeworlds' (Cope & Kalantzis, 1995; see also Ancess, 2003) and virtual, media and physical cultures inhabited by students outside the school gates:

- The teachers are really funny and have good teaching methods which keep us interested (GHSV F 19/16).

- Because my school is very multicultural, there is an understanding of other cultures amongst students (GHSV F 41/16/Sri Lankan).

- School is a comfortable place ... you can tell the teachers try their hardest, which is nice to know they care. The only real pressure is that you have to do well but the teachers generally try to help you along the way, which is good (GHSV F 178/16).

- School is great if you have teachers who can both teach and entertain ... It is great to be able to have achievements and sometimes failure. It is the experience which makes it worthwhile (GHSV M 183/16).

Thus the above students' comments point to the significance of what has been termed in the literature on effective schooling (Slee at al, 1998) as productive pedagogies and communities of commitment (Ancess, 2003; Lingard, B, Hayes, D, Mills, M & Christie, P, 2003).

PRODUCTIVE SCHOOLS, PRODUCTIVE PEDAGOGIES AND TEACHER THRESHOLD KNOWLEDGE

Martin claims that improving the quality of school life for both boys and girls at school needs to involve:

Assisting teachers in dealing with diversity, promoting active learning, developing students' higher order thinking, creating effective learning zones, providing effective feedback to students, developing good relationships with students, engaging in productive pedagogy, listening to and valuing student perspectives (2002: 37).

He also states that students value school more when 'they see its relevance to them and to the world more generally' (2002: 37). This is consistent with the productive pedagogies model of leadership and effective schooling with its emphasis on teacher threshold knowledges (see Lingard, B, Hayes, D, Mills, M & Christie, P, 2003). Such a model places quality pedagogy at the centre of any educational reform designed to enhance learning and social outcomes for students. Productive pedagogies relate to those dimensions of classroom practice that are considered necessary for producing improved and more equitable student outcomes (Lingard, B, Hayes, D, Mills, M & Christie, P, 2003). This model of pedagogy is developed from that elaborated by Newmann and Associates' (1996) research in the US on authentic pedagogy and authentic achievement and provides some indications of the character of effective pedagogies. These include a high degree of intellectual quality, high levels of connectedness in terms of curriculum content and its application to the students' lives outside of school, supportive classroom environments where students feel valued and are encouraged to take risks in their learning, along with a strong recognition and celebration of difference (Lingard, B, Hayes, D, Mills, M & Christie, P, 2003; Lingard et al., 2000). Teacher threshold knowledges are those considered necessary to be able to execute such pedagogies and relate to subject discipline knowledge, knowledge of student development, understandings about the purposes of schooling, knowledge of educational policy, as well as a knowledge and understanding of gender concepts and their impact on students' attitudes and learning (see Martino et al., 2004).

In short, this book has been written to assist schools to find ways of incorporating student voice into professional development forums as an instance of building teacher threshold knowledge about gender concepts and how they impact on students' experiences of schooling and learning. We believe that this sort of knowledge needs to inform the development and recasting of school-based policies, implementation of curriculum and the execution of pedagogical practice and pastoral care programs designed to address more effectively the educational and social needs of both boys and girls at school. This is consistent with Ancess' focus on creating communities of commitment in schools built around a 'common ethos and vision, caring and caregiving, a willingness and capacity to deal with the struggle to improve learning for disadvantaged groups of students and a striving for 'mutual accountability among all community members' (2003: 9). The building blocks for creating such school cultures and communities are 'trusting, horizontal relations, not formal externally imposed regulations and hierarchies' (2003: 3). Developing such communities also means that certain conditions for communication need to be created and nurtured, which require a commitment to involving students in the school's decision-making processes. Moreover, Ancess stipulates that such forms of communication mean 'individuals are in the habit of giving rise to their voice, expressing their ideas' (2003: 4).

At the heart of such communities is a certain practice of caring that is manifested 'when teachers use their in and out of classroom relationships with students to catalyse, induce, and sustain student engagement and facilitate responsiveness to curriculum tasks' (Ancess, 2003: 9). This also involves a 'commitment to students who have been marginalised and have adopted habits of alienation' (2003: 11; see also Martino, 2003). We argue that creating spaces in schools for students' voices to be heard is one of the first steps in building such communities. It is also necessary to create a threshold knowledge about students' lives and peer group cultures outside of the classroom that is required to interrogate the limits of common sense and naturalised gender regimes (see Gilbert & Taylor, 1991; Hey, 1997; Pallotta-Chiarolli, 1998; Haag, 1999; Martino & Pallotta-Chiarolli, 2001). Understanding the impact of these cultures, coupled with a deep knowledge about the effects of hierarchical power relationships and formally imposed regulations that often characterise teacher/student relations in schools within a 'culture of coercive compliance', is what is needed (Ancess, 2003: 1).

Creating the opportunities in schools to listen to student voices and then to use those voices to build a 'community of commitment' means actively finding ways to interrogate and to destabilise certain forms of hierarchical power – both at the whole school level in terms of teacher/student relationships and at the micro level with regards to peer group social hierarchies that are organised around what it means to be really 'cool' and 'normal' and a pecking order of masculinities and femininities. It is such school communities that have the capacity to foster the following student attitudes to schooling:

- I reckon school time is the best part of my life ... the only deal we have is to study and do the best (GHSV M 191/15).

- When I wake up I don't feel worried or nervous, just ready to attend and learn (SSGS 100/16).

- For me school is an adventure (GHSV M 50/16).

References

AAUW Educational Foundation (2001) *Hostile hallways: Bullying, teasing and sexual harassment in school*. Washington DC: American Association of University Women Educational Foundation.
AAUW Legal Advocacy Fund (2000) *A licence for bias: Sex discrimination, schools and title IX*. Washington DC: American Association of University Women Legal Advocacy Fund.
Alloway, N (1995) *Foundation stones: The construction of gender in early childhood*. Melbourne: Curriculum Corporation.
Alloway, N (2000) *Just kidding: Sex-based harassment at school*. Sydney: New South Wales Department of Education and Training: Student Services and Equity Programs.
Alloway, N & Gilbert, P (1997) Boys and literacy: Lessons from Australia, *Gender and Education* 9(1): 49–58.
Ancess, J (2003) *Beating the odds: High schools as communities of commitment*. New York & London: Teachers' College Press.
Aveling, N (1998) Aboriginal studies: For whom? And to what ends?, *Discourse: Studies in the Cultural Politics of Education* 19(3): 301–14.
Beckett, L (ed.) (1998) *Everyone is special! A handbook for teachers on sexuality education*. Brisbane: Association of Women Educators.
Blackmore, J (1999) *Troubling women: Feminism, leadership and educational change*. Buckingham: Open University Press.
Blackmore, J, Kenway, J, Wills, S & Rennie, L (1996) Putting up with the put down? Girls, boys, power and sexual harassment, in L Laskey & C Beavis (eds) *Schooling & sexualities: Teaching for a positive sexuality*. Geelong, Victoria: Deakin University Centre for Education and Change.
Boulden, K (1996) Keeping a straight face: School, students, and homosexuality – Part 2, in L Laskey & C Beavis (eds) *Schooling & sexualities: Teaching for a positive sexuality*. Geelong, Victoria: Deakin University Centre for Education and Change.
Bourdieu, P (1986) The forms of capital, in J Richardson (ed.) *Handbook of theory and research for the sociology of education*. New York: Greenwood Press.
Butler, J (1996) The poof paradox: Homonegativity and silencing in three Hobart high schools, in L Laskey & C Beavis (eds) *Schooling & sexualities*. Geelong, Victoria: Deakin University Centre for Education and Change.
Canaan, J. (1991). Is 'doing nothing' just boys' play? Integrating feminist and cultural

studies perspectives on working-class young men's masculinity, in Franklin, S, Lury, C & Stacey, J (eds) *Off-centre: Feminism and cultural studies*. London: HarperCollins.

Carrington, V & Luke, A (2002) Reading, houses and families: From postmodern to modern?, in A van Kleeck, SA Stahl & EB Bauer (eds) *On reading to children: Parents and teachers*. Mahwah, NJ: Erlbaum.

Collins C, Batten, M, Ainley, J & Getty, C (1996) *Gender and school education*. Canberra: Australian Council for Educational Research.

Collins, C, Kenway, J, & McLeod, J (2000) *Factors influencing the educational performance of males and females in school and their initial destinations after leaving school*. Canberra: Department of Education, Training and Youth Affairs.

Connell, R (1995) *Masculinities*. Sydney: Allen & Unwin.

Connell, RW (1989) Cool guys, swots and wimps: The interplay of masculinity and education, *Oxford Review of Education* 15(3): 291–303.

Connell, RW (1987) *Gender and power: Society, the person and sexual politics*. Cambridge: Polity Press.

Cope, B & Kalantzis, M (1995) Why literacy pedagogy has to change, *Education Australia* 30: 8–11.

Davies, B (1989) *Frogs and snails and feminist tales*. Sydney: Allen & Unwin.

Davison, K (2000) Masculinities, sexualities and the student body: Sorting gender identities in school, in C James (ed.) *Experiencing difference*. Halifax: Fernwood.

Day, K, Gough, B & McFadden, M (2004) 'Warning! Alcohol can seriously damage your feminine health' A discourse analysis of recent British newspaper coverage of women and drinking, *Feminist Media Studies* 4(2): 165–83.

Diorio, J & Munro, J (2000) Doing harm in the name of protection: Menstruation as a topic for sex education, *Gender and Education* 12(3): 347–65.

Dorais, M (2004) *Dead boys can't dance: Sexual orientation, masculinity and suicide*. Montreal & Kingston: McGill-Queens University Press.

du Toit, K (2003) The pussification of the Western male, <http://kimdutoit.com/dr/essays.php?id=P2327>.

Duncan, N (2004) It's important to be nice, but it's nicer to be important: Girls, popularity and sexual competition, *Sex Education* 4(2): 137–52.

Duncan, N (1999) *Sexual bullying: Gender conflict and pupil culture in secondary schools*. London & New York: Routledge.

Education Review Office (1999) *The achievement of boys*, no. 3, New Zealand Government Department for Education.

Epstein, D (1997) Boyz' own stories: Masculinities and sexualities in schools, *Gender and Education* 9(1): 105–15.

Epstein, D, Elwood, J, Hey, V & Maw, J (eds) (1998) *Failing boys? Issues in gender and achievement*. Buckingham: Open University Press.

Epstein, D & Johnson, R (1998) *Schooling sexualities*. Buckingham: Open University Press.

Faludi, S (1991) *Backlash: The undeclared war against women*. London: Vintage.

Fausto-Sterling, A (2000) *Sexing the body: Gender politics and the construction of sexuality*. New York: Basic Books.

Ferfolja, T (1998) Australian lesbian teachers: A reflection of homophobic harassment of high school teachers in New South Wales government schools, *Gender and Education* 10(4): 401–15.

Fine, M (1998) Sexuality, schooling and adolescent females: The missing discourse of desire, *Harvard Educational Review* 58: 29–53.

Fine, M & Weis, L (2003) *Silenced voices and extraordinary conversations*. New York &

London: Teachers' College Press.

Fitzclarence, L, Warren, C & Laskey, L (1996) Schools, sexuality and violence: A case for changing direction, in L Laskey & C Beavis (eds) *Schooling & sexualities*. Geelong, Victoria: Deakin University Centre for Education and Change.

Foster, V (1998) Education: A site of desire and threat for Australian girls, in A Mackinnon, A Prentice & I Elgqvist-Saltzmann (eds) *Education into the twenty-first century: Dangerous terrain for women?* London: Falmer Press.

Foster, V, Kimmel, M & Skelton, C (2001) What about the boys? An overview of the debates, in W Martino & B Meyenn (eds) *What about the boys? Issues of masculinity and schooling*. Buckingham: Open University Press.

Foucault, M (1978) *The history of sexuality: Volume 1*. Trans. R Hurley. New York: Vintage.

Francis, B (2000) *Boys, girls and achievement: Addressing the classroom issues*. London & New York: Routledge/Falmer.

Francis, B (1999) Lads, lasses and (New) Labour: 14–16-year-old students' responses to the 'laddish behaviour and boys' underachievement' debate, *British Journal of the Sociology of Education* 20(3): 355–71.

Frank, B (1987) Hegemonic heterosexual masculinity, *Studies in Political Economy* 24: 159–70.

Frank, B (1993) Straight/strait jackets for masculinity: Educating for real men, *Atlantis* 18(1 & 2): 47–59.

Gaztambide-Fernandez, RA, Harding, Heather A & Sorde-Marti, T (2004) *Cultural studies and education: Perspectives on theory, methodology, and practice*. Harvard: Harvard Publishing Group.

Gilbert, P & Taylor, S (1991) *Fashioning the feminine: Girls, popular culture and schooling*. Sydney: Allen & Unwin.

Gilbert, R & Gilbert, P (1998) *Masculinity goes to school*. Sydney: Allen & Unwin.

Goldflam, A, Chadwick, R & Brown, G (1999) *Here for life youth sexuality project*, Perth: WA AIDS Council and Gay and Lesbian Counselling Service.

Gurian, M & Henley, P (2001) *Boys and girls learn differently*. San Francisco: Jossey-Bass.

Haag, P (1999) *Voices of a generation: Teenage girls on sex, school and self*. Washington DC: AAUW.

Harding, J (1998) *Sex acts: Practices of femininity and masculinity*. London, Thousand Oaks & New Delhi: Sage.

Harris, A (1999) Everything a teenage girl should know: Adolescence and the production of femininity, *Women's Studies Journal* 15(2): 111–24.

Harris, A (2004) *Future girl: Young women in the twenty-first century*. South Yarra, Victoria: Palgrave Macmillan.

Harris, A, Aapola, S & Gonick, M (2000) Doing it differently: Young women managing heterosexuality in Australia, Finland and Canada, *Journal of Youth Studies* 3(4): 373–88.

Hey, V (1997) *The company she keeps*. Buckingham: Open University Press.

Hey, V, Creese, A, Daniels, H, Fielding, S & Leonard, D (2001) 'Sad, bad or sexy boys': girls' talk in and out of the classroom, in W Martino & B Meyenn (eds) *What about the boys? Issues of masculinity in schools*. Buckingham: Open University Press.

Hoff Sommers, C (2000) The war against boys, *The Atlantic Monthly* 285(5): 59–74.

Holland, J, Ramazanoglu, C, Sharpe, S & Thomson, R (1998) *The male in the head: Young people, heterosexuality and power*. London: Tufnell Press.

House of Representatives Standing Committee on Education and Training (2002) *Boys'

education: Getting it right. Canberra: Commonwealth Government.
Hulse, D (1997) *Brad and Cory: A study of middle school boys*. Hunting Valley, Ohio: University School Press.
Hunter, I (1994) *Rethinking the school: Subjectivity, bureaucracy, criticism*. Sydney: Allen & Unwin.
Jackson, C & Smith, D (2000) Poles apart? An exploration of single-sex and mixed-sex educational environments in Australia and England, *Educational Studies* 26(4): 409–22.
Jackson, D (1998) Breaking out of the binary trap: Boys' underachievement, schooling and gender relations, in D Epstein, J Elwood, V Hey & J Maw (eds), *Failing boys?* Buckingham: Open University Press.
Kehily, M, Mac an Ghaill, M, Epstein, D & Redman, P (2002) Private girls and public worlds: Producing femininities in primary school, *Discourse* 23(2): 167–77.
Kehily, M & Nayak, A (1997) 'Lads and laughter': Humour and the production of heterosexual hierarchies, *Gender and Education* 9(1): 69–87.
Kendall, C (1996) Homophobia as an issue of sex discrimination: Lesbian and gay equality and the systemic effects of forced invisibility, *E Law – Murdoch University Electronic Journal of Law* 3(3), <http://www.murdoch.edu.au/elaw/issues/v3n3/kendall.html>.
Kendall, C & Walker, S (1998) Combating lesbian and gay youth suicide and HIV/AIDS transmission rates: An examination of possible education strategies in Western Australian high schools in light of prevailing state statutes, *E Law – Murdoch University Electronic Journal of Law* 5(4), <http://www.murdoch.edu.au/elaw/v5n4/kendall54_text.html>.
Kenway, J (1995) Masculinities in schools: Under siege, on the defensive and under reconstruction?, *Discourse: Studies in the Cultural Politics of Education* 16(1): 59–79.
Kenway, J & Willis, S with Blackmore, J & Rennie, L (1997) *Answering back: Girls, boys and feminism in schools*. Sydney: Allen & Unwin.
Kessler, S, Ashenden, DJ, Connell, RW & Dowsett, GW (1985) Gender relations in secondary schooling, *Sociology of Education* 58: 34–48.
Kleinfield, J (1998) *The myth that schools shortchange girls: Social science in the service of deception*. Report prepared for The Women's Freedom Network, May, University of Alaska, Fairbanks.
Laqueur, T (1990) *Making sex: Body and gender from the Greeks to Freud*. Cambridge, Mass.: Harvard University Press.
Laskey, L & Beavis, C (1996) *Schooling & sexualities: Teaching for a positive sexuality*. Geelong, Victoria: Deakin University Centre for Education and Change.
Lather, P (1990) *Feminist research in education: Within/against*. Geelong, Victoria: Deakin University.
Le Compte, M (1993) A framework for hearing silence: What does telling stories mean when we are supposed to be doing science?, in D McLaughlin & WG Tierney (eds) *Naming silenced lives: Personal narratives and processes of educational change*, New York: Routledge.
Lee, V (1998) Is single-sex secondary schooling a solution to the problem of gender inequity?, in AAUW Educational Foundation, *Separated by sex: A critical look at single-sex education for girls,* Washington DC: American Association of University Women Educational Foundation, pp. 45–56.
Lees, S (1993) *Sugar and spice: Sexuality and adolescent girls*. London: Penguin Books.
Lesko, N (2000) *Act your age! A cultural construction of adolescence*. New York & London: Routledge/Falmer.

Letts, W. & Sears, J. (1999) (eds) *Queering Elementary Education*. Colorado: Rowan & Littlefield.
Lingard, B. (2003) Where to in gender policy in education after recuperative masculinity politics, *International Journal of Inclusive Education* 7(1): 33–56.
Lingard, B & Douglas, P (1999) *Men engaging feminisms: Profeminism, backlashes and schooling*. Buckingham: Open University Press.
Lingard, B, Hayes, D, Mills, M & Christie, P (2003) *Leading learning: Making hope practical in schools*. Maidenhead & Philadelphia: Open University Press.
Lingard, B, Martino, W, Mills, M & Bahr, M (2003) *Addressing the educational needs of boys*. Canberra: Department of Education, Science and Training, <http://www.dest.gov.au/schools/publications/2002/boyseducation/index.htm>.
Lingard, B, Mills, M & Hayes, D (2000) Teachers, school reform and social justice: Challenging research and practice, *The Australian Educational Researcher* 27(3): 99–115.
Lipkin, A (1999) *Understanding homosexuality: Changing schools*. Boulder, Colorado: Westview Press.
Mac an Ghaill, M (2000) Rethinking (male) gendered sexualities in education: What about the British heteros?, *Journal of Men's Studies* 8(2): 195–212.
Mac an Ghaill, M (1994) *The making of men*. Buckingham: Open University Press.
McLeod, J (2002) Working out intimacy: Young people and friendship in an age of reflexivity, *Discourse* 23(2): 211–26.
McNinch, J & Cronin, M (2004) *I could not speak my heart: Education and social justice for gay and lesbian youth*. Regina, Saskatchewan: Canadian Plains Research Centre, University of Regina.
Mahony, P (1998) Girls will be girls and boys will be first, in D Epstein, J Elwood, V Hey & J Maw (eds) *Failing boys?* Buckingham: Open University Press.
Martin, A (2002) Improving the educational outcomes of boys (Report). Canberra: ACT Department of Education, Youth and Family Services.
Martino, W (1999) 'Cool boys', 'party animals', 'squids' and 'poofters': Interrogating the dynamics and politics of adolescent masculinities in school, *British Journal of the Sociology of Education* 20(2): 239–63.
Martino, W (1998) 'Dickheads', 'poofs', 'try hards' and 'losers': Critical literacy for boys in the English classroom, *English in Aotearoa* (New Zealand Association for the Teaching of English) 25: 31–57.
Martino, W (2000) Policing masculinities: Investigating the role of homophobia and heteronormativity in the lives of adolescent boys at school, *The Journal of Men's Studies* 8(2): 213–36.
Martino, W (2001) Powerful people aren't usually real kind, friendly, open people!' Boys interrogating masculinities in schools, in Martino, W & Meyenn, B (eds) *What about the boys? Issues of masculinity and schooling*, Birmingham: Open University Press.
Martino, W (2003) 'We just get really fired up': Indigenous boys, masculinities and schooling, *Discourse* 24(2): 158–72.
Martino, W & Meyenn, B (eds) (2001) *What about the boys? Issues of masculinity and schooling*, Buckingham: Open University Press.
Martino, W, Lingard, B & Mills, M (2004) Issues in boys' education: A question of teacher threshold knowledge, *Gender and Education* 16(4): 437–54.
Martino, W & Beckett, L (2004) Schooling the gendered body in health and physical education: Interrogating teachers' perspectives. *Sport, Education & Society* 9(2): 239–51.
Martino, W & Pallotta-Chiarolli, M (eds) (2001) *Boys' stuff: Boys talking about what*

matters. Sydney: Allen & Unwin.
Martino, W & Pallotta-Chiarolli, M (2003) *So what's a boy? Addressing issues of masculinity and schooling*. Maidenhead: Open University Press.
Messner, M (1997) *Politics of masculinities: Men in movements*. Thousand Oaks: Sage.
Mills, M (2001) *Challenging violence in schools: An issue of masculinities*. Buckingham: Open University Press.
Mills, M (2004) Male teachers, homophobia, misogyny and teacher education, *Teaching Education* 15(1): 27–39.
Mills, M (2003) Shaping the boys' agenda: The backlash blockbusters, *International Journal of Inclusive Education* 7: 57–73.
Nayak, A & Kehily, M (1996) Playing it straight: Masculinities, homophobias and schooling, *Journal of Gender Studies* 5(2): 211–30.
Newmann & Associates (1996) *Authentic achievement: Restructuring schools for intellectual quality*. San Francisco: Jossey-Bass.
Nickson, A (1996) Keeping a straight face: Schools, students and homosexuality – Part 1, in L Laskey & C Beavis (eds) *Schooling & sexualities*. Geelong, Victoria: Deakin University Centre for Education and Change.
Pallotta-Chiarolli, M (forthcoming, 2005a) *Border sexualities, border families in schools*. New York: Rowman & Littlefield.
Pallotta-Chiarolli, M (2000) 'Coming out/going home': Australian girls and young women interrogating racism and heterosexism, in J McLeod & K Malone (eds) *Researching youth*. Hobart: Australian Clearinghouse for Youth Studies.
Pallotta-Chiarolli, M (ed.) (1998) *Girls talk: Young women speak their hearts and minds*. Sydney: Finch Publishing.
Pallotta-Chiarolli, M (1997) We want to address boys' education but ... *Curriculum Perspectives* 17(1): 65–68.
Pallotta-Chiarolli, M (2005b) *When our children come out: How to support gay, lesbian, bisexual and transgendered young people*. Sydney: Finch Publishing.
Petersen, A (2000) *Unmasking the masculine: 'Men' and 'identity' in a sceptical age*. London, Thousand Oaks & New Delhi: Sage.
Plummer, D (1999) *One of the boys: Masculinity, homophobia, and modern manhood*. New York: Harrington Park Press.
Quinlivan, K (1999) 'You have to be pretty, you have to be slim and you have to be heterosexual, I think': The operation and disruption of heteronormalising processes within the peer culture of two single sex girls' high schools in New Zealand, *Women's Studies Journal* 15(2): 51–70.
Reay, D (2001) 'Spice Girls', 'Nice Girls', 'Girlies' and 'Tomboys': Gender discourses, girls' cultures and femininities in the primary classroom, *Gender and Education* 13(2): 153–66.
Rees, T (1999) *Mainstreaming equality in the European Union*. New York: Routledge.
Rennie, L & Parker, L (1997) Students' and teachers' perceptions of single-sex and mixed-sex mathematics classes, *Mathematics Education Research Journal* 9(3): 257–73.
Renold, E (2003) 'If you don't kiss me, you're dumped': Boys, boyfriends and heterosexualised masculinities in the primary school. *Educational Review* 55(2): 179–94.
Renold, E (2001a) Learning the 'hard' way: Boys, hegemonic masculinity and the negotiation of learner identities in the primary school, *British Journal of the Sociology of Education* 22(3): 369–85.
Renold, E (2001b) 'Square girls', Femininity and the negotiation of academic success in the primary school, *British Educational Research Journal* 27(5): 577–88.
Rich, A (1980) Compulsory heterosexuality and lesbian experience, *Signs* 54, 631–60.

REFERENCES

Robinson, K (2000) 'Great tits, miss!' The silencing of male students' sexual harassment of female teachers in secondary schools: A focus on gendered authority, *Discourse* 21(1), 75–90.

Salisbury, J & Jackson, D (1996) *Challenging macho values: Practical ways of working with adolescent boys*. London: The Falmer Press.

Skelton, C (1998) Feminism and research into masculinities and schooling, *Gender and Education* 10(2): 217–27.

Skelton, C (2001) *Schooling the boys: Masculinities and primary education*. Buckingham: Open University Press.

Slee, R, Weiner, G & Tomlinson, S (1998) *School effectiveness for whom?* London: The Falmer Press.

Spender, D (1982) *Invisible women: The schooling scandal*. London: Writers and Readers.

Steinberg, DL, Epstein, D & Johnson, R (1997) *Border patrols: Policing the boundaries of heterosexuality*. London: Cassell.

Steiner-Adair, C (1991) When the body speaks: Girls, eating disorders, and psychotherapy, in C Gilligan, A Rogers & D Tolman (eds) *Women, girls and psychotherapy: Reframing resistance*, Binghamton, NY: Haworth Press.

Sukhnandan, L, Lee, B & Kelleher, S (2000) An investigation into gender differences in achievement: Phase 2: School and classroom strategies. London: National Foundation for Educational Research.

Swain, J (2003) How young schoolboys become somebody: The role of the body in the construction of masculinity, British Journal of Sociology of Education 24(3): 299–314.

Symes, C & Meadmore, D (1996) Force of habit: The school uniform as a body of knowledge, in E McWilliam & PG Taylor (eds) *Pedagogy, technology, and the body*. New York: Peter Lang.

Tanenbaum, L (2002) *Catfight: Why women compete with each other*. New York: Seven Stories Press.

Teese, R, Davies, M, Charlton, M & Polesel, J (1997) *Who wins at school? Boys and girls in Australian secondary education*. Canberra: Department of Education, Employment and Training.

Teese, R & Polesel, J (2003) *Undemocratic schooling: Equity and quality in mass secondary education in Australia*. Melbourne: Melbourne University Press.

Titus, J (2004) Boy trouble: Rhetorical framing of boys' underachievement, *Discourse* 25(2), 145–69.

Tolman, D (2002) *Dilemmas of desire: Teenage girls talk about sexuality*. Cambridge: Harvard University Press.

Tolman, D (1999) Female adolescent sexuality in relational context: Beyond sexual decision making, in N Johnson, M Roberts & J Worell (eds) *Beyond appearance: A new look at adolescent girls*. Washington: American Psychological Association.

Trinh, MT (1990) Cotton and iron, in R Ferguson, M Gever, MT Trinh & C West (eds) *Out there: Marginalization and contemporary cultures*. Cambridge, Mass.: MIT Press.

Uribe, V & Harbeck, KM (1992) Addressing the needs of lesbian, gay and bisexual youth: The origins of PROJECT 10 and school-based intervention, in K Harbeck (ed.) *Coming out of the classroom closet: Gay and lesbian students, teachers and curriculum*. Binghamton, NY: Harrington Park Press.

Volman, M & ten Dam, G (1999) Equal but different: Contradictions in the development of gender identity in the 1990s, *British Journal of the Sociology of Education* 19(4): 529–45.

Walker, JC (1988) *Louts and legends*. Sydney: Allen & Unwin.

Ward, N (1995) 'Pooftah', 'Wanker', 'Girl': Homophobic harassment and violence in schools, in *Girls & Boys: Challenging Perspective, Building Partnerships: Proceedings of the Third Conference of the Ministerial Advisory Committee on Gender Equity* (Brisbane: Ministerial Advisory Committee on Gender Equity).

Weaver-Hightower, M (2003) Crossing the divide: Bridging the disjunctures between theoretically oriented and practice-oriented literature about masculinity and boys at school, *Gender and Education* 15(4): 407–23.

Weiner, GM, Arnot, M & David, M (1997) Is the future female? Female success, male disadvantage and changing gender patterns in education, in AH Halsey, P Brown, H Lauder & A Stuart-Wells (eds) *Education: Culture, economy and society*. Oxford: Oxford University Press.

White, Greer (2004) A call for a level playing field: A study of masculinity 1999–2000, PhD thesis, Brisbane: Australian Catholic University.

Wilkinson, D, Denniss, R, Macintosh, A & Hamilton, C (2004) *The conflict between private schools and public values*, Discussion paper, Canberra: The Australian Institute.

Willis, P. (1977). *Learning to labour: How working class kids get working class jobs*. Westmead: Saxon House.

Yates, L (1997) Gender equity and the boys debate: What sort of challenge is it?, *British Journal of the Sociology of Education* 18(3): 337–41.

Younger, M & Warrington, M (1996) Differential achievement of girls and boys at GCSE: Some observations from the perspective of one school, *British Journal of the Sociology of Education* 20(3): 325–42.

Younger, M, Warrington, M & Williams, J (1999) The gender gap and classroom interactions: Reality and rhetoric? *British Journal of the Sociology of Education* 17: 299–314.

Index

academic achievement   60–61, 67, 142
adolescence   26–27, 172
adult cultures   26–27
alcohol use   38
Alloway, N   163
Ancess, J   167, 181
anorexia   102–4

backlash politics   7–12, 177
balance, creating   176–79
bitchiness
   Catholic high school   22
   government high school   22, 23, 24
   problem for girls   138–42, 160
   single sex girls school   19, 20
   use of word   25–26
Bourdieu, P   145
boys
   absence of girls   41
   aggression   39
   asserting masculine superiority   127–29
   body image   84, 145
   classroom behaviour   54
   compulsory heterosexuality   40–44, 81, 83, 87, 88, 127
   dislike of school   18, 20, 21, 22, 23
   disruptive behaviour   41–42

educational needs   9, 11
educational performance   12–13
feminisation   9
hierarchies   28, 34–35
immaturity   149–50
macho image   18, 22, 83–86, 146–47
'new disadvantaged'   10–12, 14
normalisation   79–83, 91
policing masculinity   29, 80, 146
positive school experience   23, 173–74, 177–79
presence of girls   23–24, 40–41
pressure to have sex   87
rejection of hierarchical power structures   31–36
resistance to learning   79
single sex school   18–19
single sex *versus* co-education   44–46
social exclusion   21
boys' education
   agenda   9, 79
   debates   6
   parliamentary inquiry   10–12, 123
'boy turn'   6
bullying
   consequences   151–52
   homophobic   37

racial dimensions   152–57
role in normative masculinity   39, 79, 80, 83, 90
sexualised   48–49, 158
whole school approach   158

co-education
boys   44–46
Catholic high school   21–22
girls   43–44
government high school   22–24
rural government high school 20–21
Collins, C   7, 12, 14, 39
conflict, dealing with   144
conformity   175
cool, being   4, 59, 86–89, 164
questioning   171–75
counselling services   69–70

Davies, B   79
disadvantage, educational   7
discipline   45
Douglas, P   8
dress codes   32–33
drug use   38, 87, 88

eating disorders   102–4

femininity
hierarchies   28, 57–62, 106–12
'normal'   96–101
policing   20, 21, 29, 96, 101–6
transgressive   96–101
femiphobia   28
fighting   142–48, 159
Fine, M   2, 116
'fitting in'   64–66, 142
Foster, V   8
Foucault, M   17
Francis, B   54, 149–50

gay, being *see* homosexuality
gender, policing   79

gender-based hierarchies   16, 123–24, 140–41
gender differences   8–9
gender equity policy   10–11, 171
gender normalisation   79
gender reform   7–10
girls
absence of boys   19–20
acting like boys   99
attitudes towards boys   20, 21, 24
body image   19, 20, 22, 24, 96, 101–4, 106–8, 118
classroom behaviour   54
dislike of school   20, 21, 22, 23
educational performance   12–13
hierarchical femininities   106–12
influence of boys   20, 105–6, 120, 142
labelling   97–98, 100, 135
'normal' femininity   97–101, 117
peer group relations   106–12
policing femininity   20, 21, 29, 101–6
positive school experience   19, 23, 60, 71, 173–74, 177–79
preferring to be girls   148
pressure to have sex   105–6
questioning gender hierarchies 113–14, 117
resistance to authority   53–57
self-regulation   101–6, 125
sexuality   101–2, 105–6, 109–11, 114–17
policing by boys   124–27
social hierarchies   57–62
social life outside school   119
transgressive   105–6, 111
Goldflam, A   152

harassment, gender-based   124–27, 137–61
of boys   83, 88, 91
Catholic high school   22
of girls   122–36

government high school   23
perpetuating masculinity   39
rural government school   21
teachers reaction to   68–70
Harris, A   57, 65–66, 101, 111
heterosexism   29
heterosexuality, compulsory   29, 41, 81, 83, 88, 127
Hey, V   131
hierarchies, gender-based   123–24, 140–41
homophobia   79, 80–81, 90
boys harassment of girls   129–32
definition   28
single sex school   18, 80
homosexuality   18, 81, 82, 129–30, 152
Hulse, D   38, 40
humour, sexualised   18–19, 36–37
Hunter, I   32

Kenway, J   97

Lees, S   109, 124, 125–26
lesbians   129–30, 152
Lesko, N   26, 27, 172
Lingard, B   8, 10

Martin, A   179–80
masculinity
asserting superiority   127–29
crisis in   6–7
hierarchies   28, 34–35
institutionalised culture   18
normative   79–83, 90
performing heterosexual   40–44, 87
policing   29, 80, 146
transgressive   80, 81, 90
Meadmore, D   32
media, role in education debate   10
men
privilege   8
reaction to women's power   8

menstruation   57, 63–64
misogyny   79

normal, being   4–5, 164
normalisation   4–5, 18
definition   29
gender   10, 79

panopticon   17
pedagogies, productive   179–82
peer group relations
gendered dimensions   16
girls   64–66, 106–12
hierarchical   18
negative effect   22
Petersen, A   8, 9
politics, backlash   7–12, 177
power structures
authoritarian   31–36, 48, 72
hierarchical   34–35
traditional   21–22

Quinlivan, K   70

racial discrimination   152–57
racial hierarchies   58–59
Reay, D   97, 98–99, 114
Rees, T   142
Renold, E   127, 145
research process   2–3, 14–16
responsibility, students   36
risk taking behaviours   38, 87
Robinson, K   39

schools
Catholic co-educational   21–22
chosen for survey   15
culture   16, 48
gender regimes   6–7
government co-educational   22–24
as prisons   10, 33, 45, 55–56
productive   179–82
rural government   20–21
single sex boys'   18–19

single sex girls' 19–20
social dimension 23
self-regulation 5, 17
sexuality
   see also girls - sexuality
   double standard 110–11
single-sex education
   boys 18–19, 38
   girls 19–20, 43–44
social class 7, 57
social hierarchies, girls 57–62
social welfare 62
socioeconomic status 7
sport 18, 46–47, 84, 88
student-teacher relationships *see* teacher-student relationships
student voice 1–5, 14, 180, 181–82
student welfare policies
   absence of focus on bullying 163
   issues 171
   reviewing 165
   template 168–70
   whole school approach 166–67
subjects, school, gendered constructs 66–68
success, gendered constructs 66–68
suicide 19, 21, 23, 151, 152
Sukhnandan, L 14
surveillance 5, 17–18, 20, 33
survey of students
   aim 1–5
   methods 14–16

questions to ask 164
results 17, 24–25
schools chosen 15
Swain, J 145
Symes, C 32

Tanenbaum, L 139, 140
teachers
   abuses of power 31, 44
   gendered expectations 56
   male 53
   reaction to harassment 68–70
teacher-student relationships
   boys' perspectives 44–46
   Catholic high school 21–22, 44–45
   girls' perspectives 55
   government high school 22, 46
   single sex boys' school 18, 36
   single sex girls' school 19
teacher threshold knowledge 179–82
Tolman, D 111, 112, 114, 115, 116, 126
Trinh, MT 1–2

uniform, school 18, 32–33

Weaver-Hightower, M 6, 172
Weis, L 2
welfare, student *see* student welfare policies
women, equality 8